501 Tips, Strategies and Professional Secrets For Home Business Entrepreneurs

S. Denise Hoyle & Sarah J. Doyle

DEDICATION

This book is dedicated to those individuals who want to learn the tips, strategies and professional secrets that will help make their home business successful. Home businesses are what this country thrives on and we want YOU to be the next success story!

CONTENTS

1 INTRODUCTION

TIPS, STRATEGIES, AND PROFESSIONAL SECRETS FOR THE HOME BUSINESS ENTREPRENEUR is written to help you, the beginner as well as advanced book writer, book seller, and general home business enthusiast have access to all the hints and tips possible to help make your business thrive! It is impossible for each of us to have the time or money to glean information from literally thousands of books in order to find the one thing we are looking for at that time.

Throughout the 35+ years of writing, publishing and home business experience, Doyle Publishing has compiled literally hundreds of articles written on home businesses. In addition, our own experience has taught us many things through the "school of hard knocks", that we want to pass along to others in order to help get their businesses "off the ground" with as few mistakes as possible, and start seeing e-mail boxes full of orders and inquiries as quickly as possible.

As you glance through this book, you will probably find many tips that seem so simple that you'll wonder "why didn't I think of that?". It doesn't really matter

WHO thought of it -- you now know about it too! And the important part is that when you begin to apply the various tips, strategies and professional secrets that are included in this book, you will see your business begin to "take off like a rocket".

2 THE HOME BUSINESS

1. Probably 90% of the millions of people who buy information via internet or mail are not "book readers" and would never be found browsing in a book store. They are buying books and information because a highly motivated package or ad that is filled with potential benefits for them has hit a "hot" button and made them reach for the envelope and stamp or place an order from the email they've received..

2. As you're building your home business, keep in mind why buyers shop by mail or online: Convenience, privacy, specialty items not available locally, bargains sold only on a national basis, non-crowded conditions compared to shopping malls. With many people working two or more jobs to make ends meet, there literally is no time left to find parking, go from store to store to find what the customer is looking for, waiting in lines to check out, etc. What better way to shop than checking out email offers or looking at flyers and catalogs in your own home while relaxing in front of the TV or browsing websites online!

3. The easiest way to have an exclusive product to sell is to create it. The easiest product to create and produce and sell by the thousands is written information.

4. Keep a positive attitude about your home business. "You are what you think about all day long!"

5. Develop an overwhelming belief and confidence in yourself. Don't even consider defeat - YOU ARE A WINNER! Remember, whatever the mind can conceive and believe, it CAN achieve.!

6. Do you know what Apple Computer, Hershey's, Mary Kay Cosmetics and the Ford Motor Company have in common? These well-known corporations all started out as home-based businesses. In fact, more than half of all U.S. Businesses are based out of an owner's home. (Quote from http://www.sba.gov/content/home-based-businesses).

7. Don't allow others to kill your dreams. Some will automatically tell you why your idea won't work and others will dismiss your ideas with a shrug of the shoulders. Listen to your own inner voice - it sometimes will be the only intelligent voice you'll hear.

8. Instead of calling your slip-ups "mistakes", refer to them as lessons. Learn from each "lesson"; remain confident and positive and you'll accomplish the goals you've set.

9. Small opportunities are often the beginning of great enterprises. If you have an opportunity to begin a part time business of book selling, book writing, writing paid posts, creating or selling products we say "go for it!"

10. Never base your entire business on someone

else's product. This is a great idea when you're just starting out, but you should be thinking about a product or book that is YOURS. This literally cuts out the competition because you are the only one who has that particular book or product available.

11.   Most home based and internet businesses are part-time enterprises and are usually a "one person" business.   With this in mind, it is essential that each afternoon or evening you create a mini- list of what you're going to do next day. In my case, the mini-list of "to do" is for my early morning work. At 3 or 3:30 a.m. my brain is not ready to "sort out" work that should be done - so if I know exactly what to do when I get in the office I can get a lot accomplished before 6 o'clock.

12. A book or manual can quite often cost less than a dollar if printed in quantity and can be sold for $15 to $25. The home business/internet entrepreneur is making a hefty profit (even after the advertising expenses) and the buyer is pleased with the purchase because he is buying years of knowledge, skill and experience that he needs.

13.   DON'T RUSH! Take your time to learn the business. Study the ads and marketing materials of your competitors. Do plenty of research on the "niche" you've picked out for yourself.   Patience will reward you.

14.   Articles widely sold in stores are not usually suitable for home business or internet sales, unless you can offer good quality at a much lower price.

15. Don't be fooled into thinking that offering one product or book will make you rich. It's great to START with one product, book or report, but you must have something else to sell to the customer after he or she orders your first product.

16. When picking a company name, stay away from adding "Enterprises" or "Associates" at the end of it. You'll be better offer choosing a name that it more original or creative.

17. If you and your spouse are starting a home business/internet business together, be sure each one understands their role in the business. It is imperative that each knows exactly what he or she is responsible for and that both are not trying to compete in one certain area, while another job is being left undone.

18. NEVER take in a partner in a home business (except your spouse) if it can be helped. Avoid hiring employees. A home business is a "one" or "two" person business that can easily be done by yourself or you and your spouse for a very long time before it would become necessary to have outside help. If you simply must have help try hiring freelancers online or flexible part-time local help who won't expect a portion of your profits.

19. There is no end to the variety of ways you can make money in a home or internet business. Any product, any hobby, any service can be sold by mail and the internet. The market is HUGE and the profit margins high! If you spend just a few minutes a day "thinking" about what you know, what you can do, you will soon have several ideas of what you can sell online from home.

20. With job security at a low point in America right now, there's a great temptation among employees to simply "walk off" the job and start a business of their own. NEVER, NEVER use the family savings on a risk-venture, which includes every new business. This is why a home or internet business is perfect - it can be worked part time, from a kitchen table, garage or spare bedroom, until such time that it is making more money than the regular

job. NOW you're ready to discuss with your spouse the pros and cons of leaving your job and pursuing only your home based business.

21. The Small Business Administration (SBA) is designed to help you get your business started right. There are many offices throughout the United States where you may write for information, and they have a wealth of informational booklets and publications that you may write for - and they're all FREE. (See listing of the SBA Field Offices for each state at the back of this book).

22. Home business and internet are not a type of business, but simply an effective way to market a wide variety of products and services. With determination and a willingness to learn, the average person can master the principles of marketing by mail and the internet.

23. Eighty to 90% of all home business and internet business is generated from only 10% to 20% of the customers. Therefore, treat each customer as a good friend and you will be receiving many more orders from them.

24. One key to success in the internet and mail-order is to SPECIALIZE. Don't spread your resources thin trying to cover a dozen marketing ventures at the same time. Do one thing until it becomes successful, then try your hand at other areas.

25. Do you have a great idea you'd like to pursue? Investigate it thoroughly. Great ideas can be turned into successful businesses if you have the persistence, determination, proper planning and needed funding.

26. Make a list of your attributes and strong points. Write down whatever you are exceptional at - those things

that you can do better than most people. Choose one or more of your strongest points that you would like to develop into a business. Work on the strong points to make them even stronger. Even better, do enough research to make yourself an expert!

27. Entrepreneurs have certain characteristics that separate them from people who remain 9-5 employees. Among the attributes of entrepreneurs are the willingness to take risks, ability to identify good business ideas, determination and confidence, ability to use "blinders" when necessary to be able to focus on a particular goal and exclude everything else, and a willingness to work the hours needed to succeed. Do you have the attributes of an entrepreneur?

28. The highly successful entrepreneur spends a minimum of 10-15 minutes daily THINKING about what can be done to improve the business, how to service the customers better, what short cuts can be done for time saving, etc.

29. Make sure you run a business with integrity. Honor agreements; refuse to take unfair advantage of customers; be on time for appointments; return phone calls promptly.

30. Mail-order and selling via the internet are not a "door to door" type of personal selling. However, your "salesmen" are found in your printing, your advertising, your designs, your website, your letterhead and on and on. The appearance of your written sales material and website gives the IMAGE of you and your company and if customers don't have a good image of you, they don't buy.

31. It's funny that most people who "don't have the spare time" to start a part time home business, wouldn't

ever miss their favorite TV program, or Monday night football, or sleeping in late on Saturday. This is the "spare time" that's needed to start ANY venture! Most of us know that we must make certain sacrifices in order to reach our goals.

32. Just because you are working at home doesn't mean you should become a hermit! Go out to lunch once in awhile; go to the library to do some research; make appointments with clients, etc.

33. What do all successful home business and internet entrepreneurs have in common? They all have been willing to "study" how to be successful in this area of business - learn from other successful people (35 years in the same business certainly says something about persistence and I'd for sure want to learn from them!). Successful entrepreneurs have learned not to let one advertising "flop" discourage them to the point of quitting. Successful entrepreneurs have been willing to start small and consistently keep working and plugging away as they watch their businesses grow and expand.

34. Home based businesses create an estimated 8,219 new jobs and entrepreneurial positions each day. SBA.Gov is an excellent place to check out home business opportunities and information.

35. Consistency of performance and quality of service are mandatory for a home business. Consistency removes doubts from customers' minds about your business. Nothing will destroy your business more quickly than when customers no longer trust you.

36. When needed, furnish pertinent company history and relevant experience in your field - just because you're just starting your home business doesn't take away from

the fact that you've "been sewing for your family for years", or "have been teaching the basics of computer to all new employees at your previous job". You probably have several years' experience in your particular field - let the customers know it!

37.   It appears that the growth of small businesses will continue to progress in 2014 as small businesses have generated more than 65% of the new jobs created in the U.S. since 1996. (Quote from http://www.getbusymedia.com/vital-small-business-statistics-trends-and-facts-for-2014/)

38.   DO NOT SELL YOUR PRODUCTS TOO CHEAPLY! On lower priced items, such as books for $20 or less, we suggest that you plan to make a 5 to 1 markup (for example, if your cost is $2, you sell it for $10). Remember, however that your customer MUST FEEL he is getting a PERCEIVED VALUE. The "value" is in the mind of the customer. As long as the majority of the customers feel they are getting their money's worth, your pricing will be right.

39.   The number one reason for business failure is management - or the lack of it. The lack of knowledge, experience, imagination, ambition, preparation, determination, unexpected competition and a waning of motivation. Eliminate as many entrepreneurial risks as possible at the beginning - know what you want and be determined to go for it!

40.   It has been suggested that you name your business to sound like a law firm - Jones and Brown; Smith, Young and Thompson; Thomas & Thomas. Keep it simple and easy to remember. Advantages: mail is opened first; calls are returned faster; secretaries respond quickly; and information is given more freely.

41. "Proceed cautiously in any endeavor and keep in mind that few miracles occur in any business. Rule out luck and use your ability, perseverance and judgment to utilize all attributes of a successful business person. Keep costs at a minimum, use what's available, start from home, and keep it simple." (Quote from "Selling By Mail Order," published by U.S. Small Business Administration).

42. There are 2 types of people in the home business industry - the "hobbyist" and the "business people". The "hobbyist" will try every "chain letter" opportunity that comes around, hoping that one day he'll make some money. The "hobbyist" may even find a single page report to promote and try one or two classified ads. The "business people" home business entrepreneur is serious about the business from the beginning. He can see that there is money to be made in this industry, so right away buys some books on the subject, reads articles regarding home business, subscribes to magazines like "Income Opportunities", "Spare Time Magazine", "Entrepreneur Magazine", etc., to learn all he can. He looks for items or books that he can sell that are of a true value to the customer. The serious home business/internet entrepreneur plans on being "in the business" longer than a month or two. Which type are you?

43. Home business and internet profits come from steady sales....repeat sales.....not quick in-and-out deals. Be prepared to be in business for the long run.

44. More than 38 million Americans now run full or part-time businesses from home. A new home based business is started every 12 seconds according to a www.businessforhome.org article written July 20, 2012.

45. A very wise person once said, "Make a living doing what you love to do, and you'll never have to work

another day in your life." Excellent advice!

46. Fear of failure is one of the main things holding many people back from success. The only way you can be assured of not failing is to never do anything! You need to realize that obstacles and challenges can really turn out to be great opportunities.

47. Drop shipping is the easiest way of getting started in home business. You do not have to invent anything; there is no storage of products; no inventory to buy; no books to write, etc. All you need is advertising money, some sales literature (which is normally provided by the company you'll be dealing with), and a bank account. Drop shipping is fairly simple. You select what you want to advertise, then place the classified ads or get mailing labels and send out the sales packages. When orders come in you simply keep your share of the profit and forward the rest to the company you're dealing with.

48. Entrepreneur magazine has dubbed the home business trend as "The Silent Revolution" and predicts that over 50 percent of all U.S. households will include some form of home-based business by the end of the decade.

49. Average income of home based businesses exceeds $50,000 annually - twice the average national employee salary -- with 20% earning $75,000 and more a year.

50. Need forms to incorporate your business, establish your business, make a will? Get them free from the library or do a quick google search online for them.

51. Opportunity involves risk. Successful entrepreneurs know you can't steal second base and keep your foot on first!

52.　You can turn "Reprint Rights" into RICHES! Once you purchase reprint rights to reports, you have two ways to market them:　1) you can advertise and sell them "as is", or 2) you can expand upon them, adding new material, making them bigger and better.　You can also combine several similar reports together to create a bigger, more valuable report or turn it into a "book" or "manual", which is a much more profitable "new information" product.　This can work like magic! There are many entrepreneurs and "niche" marketers online that have "reprint rights" material that you can choose from.

53.　One of the advantages of internet marketing and home business is that you can operate from anywhere you are - if you move, your home business/internet business goes right along with you!　Simply change the address on your literature - give the Post Office a change of address so any "residue" orders will find you, and you're ready to take off from your new location.

54.　The home business and internet businesses, like no other, give you the opportunity start small, spare time and build it up as slow or as fast as you are able to do. You can make your own success.

55.　You must be a prime-source of information or products to reap REALLY BIG PROFITS.　You must have complete control over what you are offering.　You must be in a position whereby nobody else can raise prices on you, cut off your supplies or change the rules.　YOU MUST BE THE BOSS!

56.　Anything you can do in return for a paycheck, you should be doing for yourself!　Think about it!　Your talents and abilities are being used to make someone else's fortune - why not use it for making your own fortune?

57. A good leader must retain a positive attitude, must have high expectations of what can be accomplished, and must get out in front, leading by example.

58. Always be on the lookout for discovering new business opportunities or improving on existing ones.

59. Management of your business combines technical and administrative skills with vision, compassion, honesty and trust. Just because you're in charge, don't feel that you have the right to boss people around like they are your slaves. You're not in business for the power trip - or if you are, you won't be for long.

60. You may be your own boss in your home business, but be sure that every single day you do at least one thing to generate new or additional business. Your home business can be a TREMENDOUS business, if you do the right things persistently.

61. There is no such thing as a "miracle system" or magic potion that will make you an instant millionaire. Providing genuine "value-for-value" is still the yardstick by which success in the free enterprise system is measured.

62. Most entrepreneurs like to be "the expert" in every aspect of their business. If you don't release this attitude, you will always be small - both personally and financially. There is always something that can be learned, if we have an open mind and a desire to learn and grow.

63. The most successful internet and mail order entrepreneurs send a mailing or email notice to their customers about every two months. For best results, your mailing piece should be changed slightly each time. Use different colored paper, or use a different bonus offer, or rearrange your items differently than the last mailing. If

the mailings look too much the same the customer won't even bother to look at it. Give a special discount on certain items on your website to your subscriber list.

64. The title you give yourself in your sales material can greatly affect the response or lack of response to your mailing. If you call yourself "sales manager", you have set up a negative thought process in the customers' mind - nobody likes to be "sold" anything; they just want to buy. If you simply call yourself "owner", you're making your business sound small and therefore could instill a lack of confidence in a small "one horse" business. We suggest that you put "president" after your name. This sounds good to the customer and makes you feel good too!

65. If you can't find something - CREATE IT! Niches aren't found at the end of rainbows - they're created by focusing and fine-tuning your ideas. New items and improved items are being created and improved every day - and they're not done by "the other guy" who's rich and famous or important. In every instance "the other guy" is someone just like you and me that have focused their ideas on "creating" or "improving". Once you start spending some time each day focusing on what could be created or what needs improving, you'll start coming up with ideas, ideas and more ideas that can be fine tuned into success.

66. Anyone with a marketable skill of any kind is in a position to become a consultant, teaching others to do what he or she does.

67. As an experienced home-business entrepreneur, you will find many opportunities to consult with beginners in this field in areas of advertising, marketing, publicity, communications or sales.

68.   Keep abreast of changing trends as far as your product or service are concerned.   Subscribe to "trade" journals in your specific field and read them!   By identifying trends you will be able to adjust your marketing strategy and keep ahead of others that are just advertising and not reading.

69.   74% of all American millionaires own their own business. The first day you start a home-based business you instantly TRIPLE your chances of financial independence -- and qualify for some of the most lucrative tax shelters available.

70.   Remember, in your home business, as well as in any business, nobody else can motivate you until you motivate yourself.

71.   To become a consultant in any field, you first must have special knowledge about that field, and a market willing to pay for it.

72.   A www.businessforhome.org/2012/07/home-based-business-in-america/ report says that a new home based business is started every 12 seconds, and that $427 BILLION per year is made by Home Based Businesses.

73.   To be a success in a home business you must be willing to work (there is no free lunch in this business); you must be willing to learn the business and then do what is needed without complaints or regrets.

74.   You must BELIEVE in the value of your product or service. Then when a prospective customer may compare your product to one of lesser quality, your sales material, which is loaded with BENEFITS, can assure them that your product is superior and worth the price.

75. If your home business doesn't seem to be making money immediately, it's because the business is growing, which takes time. If you consistently put your home business earnings back into the business, it will grow at a much faster rate than if you "spend" most of the earnings and put only small amounts back into advertising. Your home business growth is directly related to how diligent you are in "re-investing" your profits.

76. Every person has certain times of the day when you're most productive (mine is from 3:30 a.m. until 7a.m.). Plan to do the most important or more difficult tasks at this time. A particularly unpleasant task should be done during this period of time - you'll feel good about the accomplishment and can look forward to doing more pleasant things the rest of the day.

77. An internet or mail order product or book will succeed if it is unique or exclusive or appealing and can satisfy or create a desire upon the part of the purchaser.

78. If you are into crafts, don't limit your income just to the sale of your handmade products. There are other ways that you can supplement your income - make "kits" to sell that include your own patterns, teach a class at a local shop or as an adult education class, sell your original designs to magazines, write and publish your own "craft" newsletter, report or book. For additional ideas, see our book "How To Make CASH FROM YOUR CRAFTS".

79. Business got you stressed out? Get out of the house, away from everything that reminds you of business. Go visit somebody for an hour or so; go for a walk; go out to lunch; think good thoughts about yourself; listen to a motivational tape; read an inspirational book.

80. If you're an entrepreneur who ONLY promotes

what you do by the dollars you can make, you are setting yourself up for a guaranteed failure. What can you do for others? How can your product or written information help someone else? The more you can help others, the bigger your business will become.

81. During hard economic times when money is scarce, people will still buy information - especially "How To" and "Opportunity" information that could help the reader earn badly needed extra income or be able to start a part time sideline job.

82. Selling "information" by internet (websites) is making fortunes for many people. Be sure the "information" is something that cannot be found easily in stores; appeals to a large segment of the population; and can be sold for less than $50.

83. Nothing stays the same. Remain flexible in your business to adapt to changing trends, changing marketing methods, changing technology, etc., so that your business will always be "in the know" and poised for whatever changes may come your way.

84. Within each of us there is the power for everyone to accomplish MORE in life. Prosperity will only become reality when individuals have the fortitude to put CHARACTER into their lives. Remember one thing: when all is said and done in this life, what will be remembered is the life that we lived and the character we possessed!

3 HOME OFFICE

85. When selecting space in your house for an office keep in mind that the location can have a direct impact on how well you run your business. If you don't like your office you probably will spend as little time as possible there and you certainly won't get much done!

86. Is the heating and cooling system adequate in your office? If you've chosen to put the office in the garage, spring and fall weather might make working conditions okay, but summer heat and winter cold will prevent you from working in your "office" unless you make some changes.

87. By hanging your office phone on the wall you'll save valuable work space for other items that require table or desk space.

88. Add life to all of your electrical office equipment (printers, computers, copiers, fax, etc.) by the use of surge protectors.

89. Be sure the office space you select has adequate lighting. The more detailed your work is the more light you will need.

90.   When working at home in a limited space it becomes easy to make a "pile" of papers here, a "stack" of letters over there, a separate "pile" of letters to answer later, etc. Eliminate the clutter and take care of work as it comes in - answer the letters immediately, file the papers NOW, open and go through the "stack" of letters you'd saved for "later" - get the table cleaned off!   Go through those emails! Set a time EACH DAY to take care of the "will get to it later" items - and don't wait until "later"!

91.   Always make a list of "things to do" each day. Begin with the high priority items down to the least important. Mark off items as you complete the task. This will let you know that you are accomplishing something each day.

92.   Open a separate business checking account for your home business. Use this account only for business. This will make your end of year accounting much easier, in addition to knowing immediately what money is coming in and what you can spend on advertising, google ads, facebook ads, etc.

93.   Place greater emphasis on work that produces results.

94.   Make a poster to hang on your wall that says" Winners develop the habit of doing things that losers don't like to do".

95.   Stay organized by taking control of your time. Get in the habit of doing up-front planning. Stop rushing around without direction. Make written lists, review them,

assign priorities and take a fresh look occasionally at routine work. Rushers are reactors....planners are profit makers. Which do you want to be? The choice is yours.

96. Develop a standard step-by-step process for routine jobs. If you do certain things in a particular order each day, you get a "rhythm" built up which actually cuts the time for doing that particular job.

97. Keep your office organized. Know where everything is. Much time can be wasted looking for an item that could be spent in productive work.

98. Do not wait until customers' checks clear before sending out the order. In our 25+ years experience we've only had a handful of checks bounce. When that happens we write to the customer informing them that our policy is to send out orders within 48 hours, because we "assume" the checks will be good. Sometimes the customer will send back a money order with an apology; however, it usually happens that a bounced check can't be collected, in which case you have no choice but to write it off as a business expense. The alternative, holding up the order for 2-3 weeks for checks to clear will result in canceled orders, unhappy customers that will not do business from you again, and much unnecessary bookkeeping as you try to keep track of when orders came in, when the check might have cleared, and finally deciding when would be "safe" to ship the order.

99. There may be times when you receive a complaint from someone who says they ordered a product from you but never received it. The first thing you should do is check your records to see if you have a record of the order. If you show no order send a postcard or email to the person asking for more specific information if he doesn't have a money order receipt or canceled check

showing clearance through your bank. If the complaint was from someone trying to "rip you off", you probably will not hear from them again. If the customer does contact you with more information, chances are that somehow the order "fell through the cracks" and didn't get recorded or sent out. Go ahead and send out a second order and resolve to be more careful in the future.

100. Working at home can be quite lonely, particularly if you don't deal with people directly and you've been used to seeing and meeting people daily in your old "job". This is easily changed by setting aside time to socialize, perhaps by joining a club or group.

101. Zoning laws are what keep the residential areas separate from the commercial or business areas. This would limit the type of business you could run out of your home. For example, you couldn't open up a store in your house because that would require people to come in and out, which would theoretically disturb your neighbors. You can get around this by having a "free delivery service" business or mail order, which of course is all done through the mail or a website, which would also be done through the mail. It is always best to see what zone you are in and what restrictions apply to your area.

102. A "customer" list is much more valuable than an "inquiry" list. As "inquirers" purchase from you, move that name to your "customer" list. It is the "customer" list that you want to send extra mailings to as well as extra "specials" and promotions to keep them buying.

103. NEVER write telephone messages or notes on slips of paper or post-it notes - there's too big a chance of misplacing the notes or telephone numbers, and then there's the wasted time looking for misplaced items. Always keep a telephone message pad beside the phone

for the telephone numbers you need to keep, and use a to-do list for things you want to accomplish. Stay focused on the most important items on the to-do list and you will double your productivity and effectiveness.

104.   Save all the names and addresses of buyers and inquirers. When and if you accumulate 5000 of them, you can approach a professional list broker with the idea of placing your name list on the market. A 5000 name list can generate $100 a month income for you.

105.   Keep your inquirer names separate from your buyer names. It is the buyer names that you'll want to keep sending offers to every month to six weeks

106.   If you'd like to build a mailing list that you can start renting, the fastest way is to offer something for free. Make it an inexpensive report that could tie in and promote other products or books you have available. Make your FREE report useful information the customer can use. Not only can you build a list fast this way, but you might get some paying customers in the process.

107.   NEVER put "Enclosed is the information you requested" on the outside of an envelope if it was not requested. People do not like to be fooled. This tactic will hurt your sales rather than increase them.

108.   When you exercise "time management" wisely and do the right things at the right time, you are working "Smart". The less wasted time you have means more time for fun and leisure activities.

109.   If you are mailing to business firms, it'll pay you to take the trouble to get the names of the individuals in each firm.   One direct mail firm found that letters addressed to an individual within the business pulled four

times as many orders as letters addressed just to the firm.

110. Many times a customer will call with an order and want to chat about the weather and a dozen other things. This is great if you have plenty of time for chit-chat; however, we hope your business is so busy you don't have time for all the general conversations. Be courteous, but don't extend the conversation beyond "Yes, it's cold here today too" then take control of the conversation and get it back to business.

111. Make sure you have a professional looking letterhead and sales package. Copies of copies of copies that are faded and end up crooked on the page will all end up in the trash without being read.

112. Industry experts claim that taking charge or credit cards can increase a company's business from 10 to 50 percent, depending on the type of business and its clientele. In mail order the upper end of the increase would be likely, because it is MUCH EASIER for a potential customer to pick up the telephone and call in an order than to fill out the order form, find an envelope and stamp and then mail the order. If you have a website selling items and go through Pay Pal or other online "banking" service, you won't have to personally take credit cards.

113. By being a credit card merchant (being able to take charge orders from your customers) your business appears more established and has more credibility with the public because the customer feels like the bank has reviewed your business practices and is satisfied that you are an honest business citizen. This works the same way in an online business where you have a merchant account set up with an online "banking" service such as Pay Pal.

114. Make a poster to hang in your office that says
"If it's to Be...it's up to ME". Don't rely on somebody else
to bring you business, do your work or work your plan --
this is YOUR responsibility. After all, whose business is
this???

115. Many stores will rent you computer time, but
why pay when you can reserve free computer time at most
libraries? Our public library has a number of software
programs including games, educational software and word
processing software. You can spend some time working
on flyers, brochures, and other types of mailers without
having to own a computer. With an internet type of
business however, it is almost mandatory that you have a
computer, and I would venture to say that the majority of
homes in this day and time DO have a computer available
for this type of business.

116. Putting your customers' names and addresses on
the computer will make it very easy to print out labels for
additional mailings. Also you can have a "field" on each
customer record to keep track of dates of orders, amounts
of orders, etc.

117. Answer all leads promptly! If you delay, you
give the edge to your competitors.

118. If you're going to use "supplier prepared"
catalogs (such as SMC or Mail Order Associates, Inc.), it is
best to insert them in outgoing packages that you're
mailing. To mail them randomly to a mailing list will not
be profitable.

119. Supply complete product information to
inquirers - how can they buy if you've forgotten to include
the order form that contains the price, etc.

120.   Create an impression of personal interest by typing letters individually.   Keep your correspondence friendly and interesting.

121.   The more related items you have available to sell, the better your profits will be.   You must continually look for and add new items to what you currently offer.

122.   Don't be too dependent on any one source for your products and supplies.   It is best to do business with several suppliers in the event that one may not be able to deliver the goods.   An exception to this is if YOU have created your own products, books or reports.

123.   Most cities or counties require a business license to open a regular business (beauty shop, dress shop, auto repair shop, etc.).   Check to see how this applies to a home business or internet operation, or if a business license is necessary at all.

124.   You can substantially increase your sales volume if you install an 800 number.   An 800 number can be gotten at no extra expense or for a minimal monthly fee and you only pay for the calls that you receive.

125.   Set up and maintain rigid discipline for your office at home -- reasonable hours of work, good records, a workable filing system, telephone message book for returning calls, keep correspondence current.

126.   A major drawback to "working at home" is the fact that friends and family consider you to be "not working", therefore they feel free to drop by or waste your time "visiting" on the phone during your WORK HOURS. Be kind but firm when telling them that you're "working" at this time and you'll talk to them later.

127.   Install a separate telephone line into your office and have your own answering machine to take calls while you're "out of the office".

128.   In setting up your home office get good tools - typewriter, computer, fax - that will enable you to operate a professional business.   Good lighting, adequate work space and comfortable chairs are necessary.

129.   Use your money wisely when starting a home business. Keep expenses to a minimum and invest only in what you will need.   Determine where the dollars you spend will yield the most profit. For example, purchasing an additional classified ad, will yield much more profit than buying a new filing cabinet, when a used one will work just as well and will be much cheaper.

130.   Make sure your "home office" work space is private and functional. Don't let home activities interfere with your business or vice versa.

4 OFFICE EQUIPMENT

131. Computers are a NECESSITY for the serious home business entrepreneur. You will need a word processing program to keep track of mailing lists and for correspondence. You can also use your computer to create marketing campaigns and take care of your bookkeeping.

132. Did you know that many public libraries have computers available for customer use? These computers usually have many programs on them, so if you're wanting to do a flyer - check out what's available at the library. If you want to record names and addresses, take your portable drive to the library and do your work. The software is there, you will just "save" the information you've typed onto YOUR drive.

133. If you're just looking into getting a computer for your business, be sure to get "desktop publishing" applications. With the desktop publishing software you can create newsletters, advertisements, catalogs, brochures, flyers - everything a professional printer would have to be paid to do. Microsoft Office has most of the things you'd

be needing, and trial versions come pre-installed on most computers.

134. If you need a fax number you can use online electronic fax services like eFax so you don't have to invest in a fax machine.

135. If your computer has been exposed to extreme temperatures, allow it to reach room temperature before attempting to operate it to prevent thermal shock.

136. The worst enemies of a computer include smoke, heat, dust and static electricity charges, and most of all -- FOOD or LIQUID! DO NOT EAT around the computer - bits and crumbs of food that fall between the keys of the keyboard will eventually cause it to quit working. If you spill a drink on your keyboard, **immediately** turn the computer off. Then, turn the keyboard upside down over a few paper towels. Let it all drain for a few minutes. Then, with the keyboard still upside down, wipe it thoroughly with a dry paper towel. If it was a water spill, you can let the keyboard air-dry for an hour or so and it should work fine. If it was a soda or juice that dries "sticky" you may have a 50% chance of the keyboard working after it dries. If it will not work after drying, your best choice is to go get a new keyboard.

137. The "preventive maintenance" you perform on your computer will affect the operation of the computer. One simple suggestion is not to stack papers or other items close to the computer. It needs plenty of ventilation to avoid heat buildup.

138. Computer monitors, like TV screens, generate static electricity. Static in the air can become a problem for your computer, especially in the winter (remember how just walking across a carpet can create enough static to

"zap" someone, or zap yourself when you touch a door handle?) Recommended solutions are to spray diluted fabric softener on any nearby carpeting, or to place a fabric softener sheet under the keyboard.

139. Monitor screens are dust magnets. If screens are not cleaned regularly the dust will filter down into the keyboard and can also cause a dust build-up inside the computer. Clean the monitor regularly with a lint free cloth.

140. There are two kinds of leases: FINANCE LEASES which require you to purchase the equipment at the end of the lease period for a percentage of the original purchase price or for a nominal amount, and an OPERATING LEASE, in which the ownership of the equipment usually reverts to the leasing company at the term of the lease. Most leases for office equipment are "Operating" leases and payments on this type of lease are treated as an operating expense and are deducted directly from operating revenues.

141. Leases are usually very technical in nature and should be reviewed by either your accountant or attorney before you sign them.

142. One advantage of leasing equipment is that you will get 100% financing - perhaps paying only the first and last payment up front and the remainder is financed.

143. There are many available options for cell phone providers these days including no contract plans that may work just fine for your business. Be sure to compare rates and plans as well as the features of the phone.

144. When looking for a printer for your computer, look for one of the newer laser printers. You'll be able to

produce brochures, newsletters, business cards, and labels that look like they've been done by a professional printer.

145. Be sure to check with your accountant before you make any major equipment purchases. For example, if you purchase equipment for cash, you may not get to deduct the entire cost of the equipment as a business expense that year. You should perhaps choose to "lease" the equipment (and have all lease payments be deducted as a business expense) and use the CASH for additional advertising.

146. When you get to the point of needing to purchase large pieces of equipment (larger computer system, photocopier, etc.), it will probably be easier to obtain a loan from a COMMERCIAL FINANCE FIRM instead of a COMMERCIAL BANK. Reasons: A) Commercial finance firms will lend money on riskier projects than commercial banks will; B) You'll have less paperwork and red tape when dealing with a commercial finance firm; C) Commercial finance firms will require less control of your business than a commercial bank would. Disadvantage of commercial finance firms - you will be paying a higher rate of interest (perhaps 2% to 5% more).

147. Make a habit of regularly backing up your computer. If they "crash" you may lose your most valuable asset - your information. Back up your hard drive with an external drive and store the backup in a fire proof safe. In the event of a computer crash or fire, which we all hope never happens, you will have your information, customer names, books and other documents in a safe place.

148. To lower the cost of printing, consider having your printer cartridges "recharged". Check the type you

have and call several computer/printer maintenance
companies for prices of "new" compared to "recharged"
cartridges. You can also buy "reconditioned" or
"remanufactured" cartridges from most office supply
stores at a lower price than new cartridges.

149. If your business relies heavily on a computer,
you shouldn't be operating without an uninterruptible
power supply (UPS). A UPS is a sophisticated
battery/transformer that runs your computer should the
power fail. It keeps your system alive long enough to save
opened files and exit. This can save you hours of time
trying to "redo" what you already spent hours writing, and
keeps vital data from being damaged during a power surge
or outage.

150. As a protection to your computer, install a copy
of Norton Utilities. This program is valuable for
recovering damaged systems in DOS and Windows, for
restoring files and disks that were erased or reformatted by
accident, fixing corrupted files, and improving the
performance of your computer. The cost is usually around
$110 and could very well be the "cheapest" program you
can buy for the benefit it gives!

151. All-in-one printers are a smart investment as
you can also use them as scanners, copy and fax machines
while the saving the space and expense of having all four
machines.

152. If you have purchased a small copy machine or
all-in-one printer and can copy your own book pages, we
recommend that you make 10 copies at a time so you
always have some copies available, but not too to store
comfortably.

5 WRITING YOUR INFORMATION

153. To be successful in selling information/books by mail or internet you should stay away from fiction, poetry, autobiographies, etc. Good "how to" and "opportunity" books are always great sellers.

154. Consider putting together a catalog or brochure of your books and information products that you can send or hand out to interested parties, and include in any mailings or packages that you send out.

155. Your first "catalog" may not be more than a few pages printed on white paper. You can then "graduate" on to newsprint catalogs or cardstock brochures.

156. You may be surprised at how much revenue you generate simply from handing out and circulating your catalog.

157. Be sure to copyright your book if you are writing one. To obtain registration forms, write to the Register of Copyrights, U.S. Copyright Office,

Washington, D.C.20559. You will receive some forms and easy-to-follow instructions or go online to Copyright.gov to get the forms you'll need.

158. Every person knows a little about a lot of things and a lot about a few things. It is the knowledge of the "few things" that can be written into a book or report and sold. There are people everywhere who would gladly pay you for the knowledge you have on a certain subject. Think about it - what do you know that could be expanded on and written into a pamphlet or book and sold?

159. Regardless of what book or item you are promoting you must FIRST **Identify Your Market**! What customers will you target? What magazines do these people read? What websites do they visit? What category of mailing lists should be rented? (You certainly wouldn't be sending information about boats to mailing lists of "sewers and crafters")

160. Ninety percent of successful home business and internet entrepreneurs got their start by selling information. Information doesn't have to be a "book" or "manual" - it can just be one or two pages and give specific information. If you have come up with a pattern for a unique bird house, you can draw up the design and write the instructions on a one or two page information sheet and advertise it in appropriate websites and magazines and be prepared for an avalanche of orders!

161. It is our opinion that the best format for a book to sell by mail is 8.5" x 11" in size. This is the easiest size to print, whether doing it yourself or having a printer do it, and easier to mail.

162. You do not have to have a printer print your book! You can simply have your pages printed and

collated at a copy shop or Office Depot and you can do the remainder of the book binding at home with a spiral binding machine.

163. If you have a catalog (catalog of products or catalog of books), should you charge for it? There is magic in the word FREE. You will get many more requests for a catalog if it is free. The purpose of the catalog is to generate business, and we suggest in the case of catalogs "the more you tell, the more you sell!" Some catalog companies will remove the names of "inquirers" if they don't order from a couple of mailings, thus deleting those who have just ordered because it was free.

164. In thinking of a subject for writing a book, some considerations would be: a) does the subject have a strong universal appeal? b) is the audience large enough to enable you to sell a quantity of books? c) do you know enough about the subject to begin, and can do research to get additional information? d) is the prospective audience reachable by classified ads or direct mail or through Google ads?

165. Every person wanting to write a book, manual or report should become aware of firms like FedEx Kinko's, which are called "copy service centers" or simply "copy shops". Many are open 24 hours 7 days a week. They offer binding, collating, copy setting, faxing and other services. They usually also have computers set up for customers so you can even do your typing there if you don't have a computer or typewriter at home.

166. The easiest topic to write about is one you have an interest in.

167. A "test" for any book or product you want to sell would be this..... would you be willing to SELL it to a

relative, friend or neighbor. Would you be willing to stand by it in a retail outlet and say "this is my book or product" and be willing to sell it to a stranger?

168. For those writing books or reports, the general topics that will sell the best include "earning money", "self-help", and "self-improvement". "How To" and "Opportunity" books are always good.

169. If you have a "NEW" approach to an old subject or topic and can write a "how to" book about it, you may have a winner. Your initial success will hinge on the UNIQUENESS of your book. A "copy cat" won't stand out and be noticed.

170. In this day of "recycle", if you have a method of recycling or reclaiming or reusing items, you may have hit a "hot" button for many people.

171. Consider writing a "newsletter" to send to your customers. Newsletters achieve a higher rate of readership than sales letters. Part of the newsletter can be new information, tips, hints, and the other part a sales pitch for books that you have available, or other items that you offer.

172. By putting your telephone number on all sales packages, newsletters and follow-up information to your customers, you are instilling a feeling of trust in that customer. The customer doesn't know you are running your business out of a spare bedroom. The telephone number indicates a real business and real people.

173. A photo of you at work personalizes your advertising material. However keep artwork to a minimum and use it only to show benefits. NEVER use artwork in a sales letter.

174. Offer a money-back guarantee in your ads. The money back guarantee should be at least 30 to 60 days. The guarantee builds buyer confidence.

175. Consider making a "catalog" of books that would contain small pictures of each book as well as a paragraph highlighting the benefits of each book. Be sure to have an order form included on a page in the "catalog" or as a loose order form for the prospect.

176. Don't skip "study" time and "research" time. The more you know about home business, internet and book writing, the better your business will be. It is advisable to buy several books dealing with the subject of "writing" or "home business" or "advertising". Each book has various ideas and opinions that you can incorporate into your own business.

177. Stay "excited" about your book or product! The more excitement you can convey in your sales material, the better your chances are of creating a red-hot, money-producing ad or direct mail package.

178. If your "sales package" isn't getting the return orders that it should, you need to take a hard look at the sales package. Maybe the product or book needs to be presented differently. Present your product in a way that is advantageous to the customer. The sales package needs to be loaded with benefits, benefits, benefits.

179. Make a statement at the beginning of your sales letter letting the prospect know there are tidbits of help included in the letter. Make a statement like "see FREE insider tips below".

180. To get ideas of products and information that's being offered look through the advertising sections of craft

magazines, farm magazines, trade journals, and community weeklies. Many times just seeing what's out there can bring to your mind a product you can make or information you can put together in the form of a book or report and offer for sale to the public.

181. Make your sales letters communicate to the prospect - not confuse him. Keep sentences and paragraphs short. Don't ramble on and on with "and's". Write in the same manner that you would have a conversation with a friend.

182. Direct mail writing is actually "selling". You cannot sell anything if the sales message is hard to follow and hard to understand.

183. When looking through classified ads in various magazines, you'll want to send for reports, "details" and other materials to get ideas of how other home business dealers do their writing, promoting and advertising. If some ad calls for $1 for details or $2 for information, NEVER enclose cash in the envelope. Either send a check (which can be written off as a tax deduction) or enclose unused postage stamps (which, of course, are written off as a tax deduction).

184. The title you choose for your book or report is crucial to its success. If you have had very little success in advertising a book, try changing the title of the book - many times a title change will make sales skyrocket.

185. Read everything you can about how others are making profits with home business and book/report writing. This does not mean to COPY other people's works, just get ideas that will help improve your own business.

186. Learn to listen. Let someone read your written material for a second opinion (a college student majoring in advertising/marketing or someone who does a lot of writing as part of his job). You don't always have to DO what the person suggests, but sometimes it can make your sales letter or book/report better.

187. Insert tidbits of outright help in your sales letters and watch how fast people start getting interested in whatever you sell.

188. Don't lump tidbits of information all in one place in your sales letter - scatter them throughout the letter. Prospects will continue reading to see what other information you have for them.

189. If you are writing a book, the title should tell the prospective reader what the book is all about. If it doesn't clearly do this, you can be missing a lot of sales.

190. Use commas only for clarity. Every comma will slow the reader down for the pause, and if there are too many pauses the reader will stop reading altogether.

191. Use as many "sub-heads" as you can in your sales letters. Place the subheads either flush left or centered, and either make them all caps or underlined. People will read the subheads if they don't read anything else. If the subheads are interesting to the reader they will go back and read the paragraphs under the subheads.

192. Any lay person is free to write, lecture and otherwise render advice in general for fees as long as the advice or information is general and not offered to an individual. For example, you may write or lecture about legal matters in the abstract, but unless you are a licensed attorney, you may not counsel a person in legal matters for

a fee.

193. Write your sales material to "express" not to "impress". Who are you trying to impress? An English teacher? No! You're trying to make a sale and you can do that best if you keep a few basics in mind. A) Use short, everyday words; B) Keep sentences short - about 15-20 words; C) Keep paragraphs down to about 3-4 lines (not 3-4 sentences, but LINES). The easier your material is to read and understand, the bigger the possibility for a sale.

194. Use plenty of subheads. As a general rule, people tend to glance at the bold statements rather than "read" the entire sales letter. If your heading and subheads "jump" out at them and catch their interest, your material will be read.

195. Use quotations frequently in your sales material. People love to see what others have to say about your product or service. They can relate to other customers easier than believing your convincing sales statements.

196. NEVER leave off the P.S. at the bottom of your sales letter. This is the last opportunity you have to drive home a sales point that could be the clincher that makes the sale! (P.S. - you don't have to limit yourself to just one P.S., use two or three if you want to make several final statements!)

197. Inserts in a sales package can dramatically increase the responses. For example, if you' re selling books, you might enclose a small insert headlined: **"EXCERPT FROM A TYPICAL PAGE"**. Then quote, word for word, a few paragraphs from the most exciting part of the book.

198. One way to hold the reader's interest is to write

notes in the margins of the sales letter. You might write "don't miss this" and draw an arrow pointing to the paragraph, or "look at this". These notes must be written legibly and make sure they are the same color as your signature so they will look like you've gone along and personalized the letter especially for that one reader.

199. By putting your bank reference somewhere in your mailing, prospective customers will have more confidence is your business.

200. After writing your book ask two or three people to proof-read your manuscript for consistency, spelling, word usage and punctuation. Don't rely on your computer "spell check" to detect all errors - you could have typed in "work" instead of "word" and it would be spelled right and be totally WRONG! Also, re-read your own manuscript to see if it actually says what you want it to say.

201. A good method to getting your sales letters read all the way through is to never end a page with a complete sentence. Arrange your material so that you have to cut a paragraph or sentence at the bottom of the page and write "over" or "Turn Page" or "Next page" at the bottom. A general rule to remember is that people typically don't do anything on their own - you must tell them. They may quit reading the sales letter at the bottom of the first page without ever turning it over, so if you make the decision for them to continue reading, your sales will increase tremendously.

202. Libraries devote considerable funds and staff to their reference functions. The reference staff knows where to go to get information you want and can direct you to various resource books that you'll need. Don't overlook this most important place of information!

203. The SBA (Small Business Bureau) produces and maintains a library of management assistance publications, videos and more. A complete listing of these products is available in The Small Business Directory. Call 1-800-8-ASK-SBA and ask for a copy or visit their website at sba.gov.

204. Additional information on assorted topics for book writing can be ordered through the Government Printing Office. Write to the Superintendent of Documents, U.S. Government Printing Office, Washington, DC 20402 or visit their website at gpo.gov.

205. Use contractions to make your letters "personal". After all, you wouldn't say "you will" in a general conversation - you'd say "you'll". Also you wouldn't say "I would" - you'd say "I'd". Write like you are speaking to the individual and you'll get better results.

206. Your own catalog is the BEST way to sell more and more products! For around $500 you can come up with a nice catalog printed on "news print" (like the daily newspapers), which can be folded into a 5" x 7" size for mailing. Catalogs of this type are cheaper to make than a large number of single flyers or circulars.

207. Don't get carried away with choosing a fancy parchment type paper for your sales letters. In general, customers are not going to evaluate the paper type - they will be evaluating the CONTENT of your letter and sales material.

208. When making a catalog of your products be sure to use testimonials throughout the catalog from satisfied customers.

209. Always put your best sellers in the front of your

catalog.

210. If you're sending out a catalog, it would be wise to add a few lines at the bottom of the order form asking your customers to recommend friends who would like to receive one of your catalogs. Make room for your customer to write out the name and address of two or three friends.

211. If ever you doubt that your "how to" information would be of value to someone else, just spend a few minutes at your local magazine stand. Look at the covers of the magazines and observe how many feature article titles include the words "How To........". The how to's are endless. They repeat month after month, year after year and those "how to" titles SELL magazines. They'll also sell your information whether in book or report form!

6 ADVERTISING

212.   Use "mini-flyers" as an inexpensive method of advertising. Mini-flyers (see example) can be made 10 to a page and printed on bright colored paper. Cut them apart and put one in every bill that you pay (gas bill, telephone bill, Sears, etc.). Somebody at each office has the boring job of opening those letters all day long, and your mini-flyer will probably be read then passed around the office. Remember, most bills come to you with offers printed on the envelopes and additional offers inside with the bill.

213.   It is imperative that direct mail packages be stuffed so that when they are opened from the back, the first thing the prospect sees is the "headline" of your letter. You want the prospect to read "Dear Friend" as he pulls the information out of the envelope.

214.   ALWAYS   fold   each   information   piece separately, so the prospect can pick them up one at a time to read them. Never fold everything together.

215. Every advertisement must have a "key" code in order to track the number of responses from a particular advertisement. A "key" code could be an added letter to

your street address (124**A** Pine St.); a "department" number (Dept. E); a variation in the spelling of your name (Denise, Danece, Deniece, Dennis, etc.)

216. Make a copy of your advertisement to put with an advertisement record sheet (see sample at the end of this book) and place into a 3 ring binder. This binder will be used on a daily basis as you receive orders and inquiries.

217. The minute you get your mail, separate the inquiries/orders BY KEY CODE. Find each key code advertisement record sheet in a spreadsheet or a 3-ring binder and add in the "daily" totals, as well as the "to date" totals. This record sheet is the only way you'll be able to determine if an ad is making a profit.

218. If doing a direct mailing from names/labels you've rented, you should have approximately 90% of the total number of responses back to you typically from within a month of the date you received your first reply. It will take about four months before 99% of all replies will come in, as some will lay the offer aside and pick it up a month or two later and act on it.

219. Bulk mailings will take from 3 to 28 days to actually get delivered, depending on the time of year and the amount of other bulk mailings the post office is working. In addition, those letters to the states further away from you can take up to the 28 days to get "through the system" and delivered.

220. If you are mailing first class and are doing a mailing to your local area, the best day to do the mailing is on Saturday. Your letter will arrive on Monday or Tuesday and the prospect will have all week to review it. If that same letter arrived on Friday or Saturday, there's a big possibility that it will get laid aside because of weekend

events and may never get opened.

221. Is there something inherent in your product or service that you could offer as a free bonus for promptness in ordering? Perhaps you have a "report" that relates to the book that you're offering - instead of casually stating   "free report with order" in the text of the advertising flyer, make a special 1/4 page insert that states "FREE (name of report) report when you order within 10 days". Many mailers report as much as a 50% increase in orders.

222. When looking for a copywriter to do your ads, be sure the writer is someone who sells products and services, not just general informational ads.

223.   Take a large piece of paper and write down everything of interest you would list about the book or product you intend to advertise.   Determine and circle which words are the "key" words that would be most likely to motivate the reader. Use those words in the preparation of your classified ad.

224. Once you know the facts and figures about your book or product, you must then turn them into benefits. BIG benefits is what makes red-hot sales copy!

225. Be specific in classified ads - avoid generalities. Get to the point. Be as brief as possible, making the ad clear and easy to understand.

226. Incorporate the reader's NEEDS and WANTS into your ad. Spell out how your product or service will satisfy those needs and wants.

227.   Always write ads in an enthusiastic personal style. Enthusiasm brings orders!

228. Make your ads "personal". Use "I" and "YOU" - but fill your ad copy with more "You" than "I". If your ad doesn't have at least twice as many you's as I's, you're offering too few benefits to your reader.

229. Good advertising copy is SIMPLE advertising! It must be easy to read and easy to understand.

230. What others say about your book or product is more convincing than what you say. Use as many testimonials as you can obtain, and if the customer permits, use their whole name.

231. Knowing WHAT you're really selling, WHO really wants it, WHY they want it, and HOW to get to them, is the secret to marketing success.

232. One of the basics of writing successful direct mail letters is to put yourself in the place of the prospect.

233. If you'll send a letter in an envelope, your chances of getting it read and acted upon improve dramatically.

234. People procrastinate. If at all possible, put a time limit on your offer -- nothing longer than a 10-day limit.

235. Try to keep up with the competition. If you know what they're doing - do yours DIFFERENT! Copycat mailings seldom work. Be creative.

236. If your product or book is not selling, consider whether or not your ad is appealing, and verify that the publication or website you run it in is the right audience for your offer. Also check to see that your ad is BELIEVABLE! Does it sound "too good to be true" that

readers will shy away from?

237. Don't waste a single word in your home business classified ad! Home business classified ads MUST produce results and do it RIGHT NOW!

238. Don't use misleading words or terms in your ads! If your potential customer does not clearly understand what you are offering, you may get a lot of inquiries, but very few orders.

239. THE FIRST THREE WORDS of your classified ad should attract the person who might be interested in your offer.

240. When writing your sales letter, ALWAYS add a P.S.. The P.S. will attract the strongest attention. Make it an intriguing sales pitch.

241. "Flexibility" is a key word for direct mailings. You are in control - you can mail when you want and to the people you choose to mail to. You can mail an entire package containing several advertising sheets and cover letter, or you can mail a single advertising flyer - the choice is yours.

242. Perseverance is a major key to success. You should be prepared to stay in business for at least a FULL YEAR in order to get things running smoothly and profitably. Keep your ads running regularly in the magazines of your choice. One or two times running an ad will not be an indication of whether or not you have a profitable business. STICK WITH IT!

243. Never start a home or Internet business unless you understand exactly what to do. If you're not clear on what to advertise, where to advertise, how to advertise,

and so on, do a little more reading of books and information on the subject. Make a plan then follow that plan!

244. When writing classified ads don't worry about building your vocabulary - concentrate on putting "everyday" conversation on paper.

245. Most successful home business entrepreneurs advertise using several methods. Test ads with a single classified ad to check the results. Test an advertising flyer with a thousand names from a mailing list. It is never a good idea to "put all your eggs in one basket" in home business. One method of advertising may pull a great many responses this month while another method doesn't do so well. Next month, it may be reversed.

246. Always "test" your classified ad before doing a full blown advertising promotion with it. Run the ad in one magazine for one or two months and keep very careful records of the results. Only if it proves to be a winner will you continue to run the ad. If it has "marginal" results, you can try re-writing the ad and doing a second test. If it is a definite bomb, check to see if you have placed it in an appropriate magazine, do a complete overhaul of the ad and try it again.

247. Because classified ads charge for every word in the ad, it is important to convey your message in as few words as possible. However, don't use so few words that the reader has no idea what you're talking about.

248. NEVER advertise in a magazine or publication that you haven't seen.

249. Some magazines don't have a regular "classified" section, but do accept small 1/2" display ads, which will

serve the same purpose as classified. Check the way the ads look to see if it is something you would want to use.

250. Use "down to earth" wording in your ads, including a little slang - this makes people warm up to you. And warm people BUY!

251. Be very careful to insure you are using the RIGHT classification heading in magazines. One home business dealer doubled his responses by merely using a different classification for his advertisement.

252. If you're anxious to get started in your business and don't want to wait the 4-6 weeks it takes for classified advertising to reach the public, try a small test by direct mail. By using mailing lists you can have your advertising flyers in the prospects' hands within a week and be getting results by the following week. You can also advertise on websites in your market or use a service like Google Adwords.

253. "Quick Turn Around" time of direct mail campaigns will let you appraise the success or failure of your advertising within a few weeks. Magazine ads could take 6 to 10 weeks to calculate results - deadlines are 4-6 weeks prior to publication and several more weeks are needed to calculate about 90% of the results.

254. Your advertising material must clearly and conspicuously show your guarantee. The guarantee should indicate whether the guarantee provides for replacement, repair or refund, and WHO is making the guarantee.

255. Remember if you are using mailing lists for your direct mail campaign, the results will depend on three things: the quality of your mailing list names, the quality and usefulness of what you are trying to sell and the quality

of the mailing literature that you're sending out.

256.   Direct mail advertising is by far the most expensive way to reach quantities of people.   Magazine classified ads range from $2 to $7 per word and a classified ad with a total cost of $150 - $200 could very well reach 350,000 or more households.

257. When writing powerful ads make sure the word "you" shows up more often than your product name.

258. Write ads whose subject is the reader and the hero is your product or service. Make the ad about your customers and their needs, then explain how your product or service is unique among all others. By stressing the benefits rather than features, your product or service will "save the day" for the customer and indeed be the "hero"!

259. In addition to classified and display advertising and direct mail, there are other ways you can sell your products. For example, you can set up a display of your books or products in a mall near you around Christmas time and watch your sales boom! In addition, if your book is one that can be sold to special groups, like business students at a college, church groups, etc., you'll be able to make extra sales by contacting each group. Check the Standard Rate & Data book at the library to get a list of book reviewers from publications in your market and send them a letter and copy of your book to review.

260. Your classified advertising must be specific. It costs too much money to mail to people who might not understand what it is that you are offering – and had they known, they wouldn't have sent for information. Be sure you give a brief accurate description of what you are offering.

261. When placing a display ad always request "right hand page" as that will be the most responsive location for your display ad. Check with the magazine to see what their policy is -- they may have a "first come, first served" basis for selecting the right hand pages, or they may charge an extra fee for you to be on a specific page. Also, the closer to the front your ad is, the better for responses.

262. There is a time of delivery rule on home business merchandise that assumes the product will be shipped within 10 days. If you determine you are unable to ship within 10 days you must advise the customer that there will be a delay, the reason for the delay and offer a new shipping date. You must also enclose a card with postage affixed on it so he may inform you whether he agrees with the delayed shipping date or wishes a refund.

263. There are "state statutes" in some states regarding home business and post office boxes. For example, in the state of California, it is illegal for a home business company to advertise in any publication using a Post Office Box as the only address. The legal name, and its street address, as well as the Post Office Box MUST appear in the advertising and on the order forms. By simply using your street address, you will not have a problem.

264. NEVER make references to your enclosures (brochure, catalog, flyer) in the middle of your letter. If you side track the reader in the middle of the letter to look elsewhere for information, they may never pick the letter back up again. The last paragraph of your letter is the best location for references to enclosures (example: "take a look now at the green flyer for all the latest information....")

265. Readers will generally "scan" the classified ad

section. With this in mind, you have under three seconds for your headline to capture the attention of the reader. If you don't have a GREAT headline, the rest of the ad won't matter because it probably won't get read by the "scanning" audience.

266. If you use a photo in your advertising make sure it gives a strong benefit to the reader. Don't just describe the photo - looking at it will explain that. Since nearly all photo captions are read, don't miss this wonderful opportunity to turn it into a selling tool!

267. Best months to advertise in are (in order) January, February, October, March, November. Worst months to advertise in are June, July, December and August. (This means the month in which the publication reaches the customer. A publication may have a "cover" date of January, but is mailed out and reaches the customers in December.)

268. After deciding which magazines you want to advertise in, write to each of them and request a "media kit". This is a pre-packaged information kit that contains advertising prices, deadlines, general information about the magazine and usually will contain a current issue of the magazine.

269. NEVER start out with a display ad. Display ads are very expensive and you could have placed 10-20 classified ads for the price of one display ad. In addition, small display ads don't give enough room to properly "sell" the item or book you're offering. Full page display ads often run $8,000 to $50,000 or more, depending on the magazine. ALWAYS use classified ads for building your business.

270. If your business is one that can be advertised

locally, make bulletin board flyers with tear-off tabs at the bottom. Print your flyer so that there is enough room along the bottom to put a row of your telephone numbers (see sample). Make as many copies of this flyer as necessary, printing it on brightly colored paper. Before hanging, clip between each of the telephone numbers so it will be easy for the reader to tear off the number in order to call you when they get home.

271. Advertising flyers should always be printed on bright paper - fluorescent paper is the best.

272. With consistent advertising, combining both classified ads and direct mail packages, over time your name will become more and more familiar to people. Whether your business is selling books, products or is service oriented, people will begin to relate to you, consider you a "friend" and will also tell others about you and your products. This "word of mouth" advertising is the best of all!

273. If there are a lot of ads out for products that are very similar to what you offer, the best way to insure that yours is purchased, put LIFE in your sales letters. Turn every sales letter into a Number One salesman! Don't just tell about your product - SELL IT! Use the words that will push the emotional buttons of your customers and trigger the sale.

274. Don't waste a single word in your classified ad. Each ad must produce results and do it with a minimal number of words. Read and re-read your ads several times and a few days later read it again. Don't be afraid to cut the ad to pieces and start again if it isn't clear and concise.

275. Remember that with classified ads, the beginning or small home business dealers are competing

equally with the large home business firms because all classifieds are displayed in the same type size and are listed by various "interest" categories.

276. Classified and website ads are the most inexpensive way to build big profits in a home business. They cost the least amount of money for numbers of inquiries and dollars in sales.

277. If you're offering a "free introductory sample" in your ad, be sure to send a strong sales message with the freebie that conveys the message "If you like what I just gave you free, just imagine how much you're going to enjoy what I have for sale".

278. NEVER ask for SASE (self addressed stamped envelope) in a classified ad or $1.00 for postage, etc. If you are offering a FREE report, or FREE information, let free BE free. By making additional stipulations to your free offer you'll cut the response by 30%-50%.

279. NEVER try to sell books directly from a classified ad. This does not work because you can't get enough information in a few words to create enough interest for the reader to order. Use the two-step advertising method. One: advertise the book and put "Free information". Two: send the inquirers an advertising flyer about the book. The advertising flyer will give enough room to tell something about the book as well as the benefits to the reader. If the benefits are clear and creates a desire in the reader, he or she will then order the book.

280. It would be good to remember that many beginners in home business lose their money mailing to "dead" or overworked mailing lists. Classified ads bring "active" and "live" prospects!

281. There is minimum risk with classified ads. You can reach thousands and millions of prospects for a few dollars and thus be able to "test" your offer in a variety of magazines.

282. A simple sign on the back of a van or on a road side sign can get your message out to hundreds of people daily. Consider putting your web address across the top of your back car window.

283. When one of your press releases gets printed in a magazine or newspaper, it would be to your advantage to write or call the editor to thank him for including your product in their publication. It would also be good to let the editor know about the good results you've had from the "free publicity". One of our press releases that had resulted in a two page story in a newspaper brought in hundreds of responses for our book. We immediately called the editor to inform him of the tremendous number of responses we'd had, and this call resulted in another paragraph in a later editorial section of that same newspaper, which brought in even more responses.

284. It generally takes 6-12 months for your business to get rolling. Be prepared to spend the time and money necessary to get the business "off the ground". Consistent advertising of your books and products will begin to pay off if you stick with it. If, after two or three months into your home business, you decide that you're not showing a profit and quit - you will indeed be the loser! You will probably be quitting just before the business starts to snowball and if you had "stuck it out" you would begin to reap huge profits from the work you'd been doing.

285. Test after test in direct mailings has proven it is the LETTER that does the selling, not the additional enclosures in the sales package. People read the letters

first because that's the personal part. If the letter hasn't generated enough interest for them to look further, the whole package will be trashed.

286. Your ads should not be so crowded with words that the type is too small to read. Just get the key facts across.

287. A wise man once said that it would be impossible to live with a person who had never failed or been defeated in any of his endeavors. This same man also discovered that people achieve successes in almost exact proportion to the extent to which they meet and master adversity and defeat.

288. Be happy that there are competitors out there! They are spending money on advertising to stimulate sales. If your flyers, direct mail pieces or classified advertising hits the customer's eyes just as all the previous advertising has convinced him/her to buy, you will get the sale. If you are persistent and consistent in your advertising, you'll get your share of the business.

289. A motto or slogan that uses a play on words to express a goal or make a point about your company is an excellent way for people to remember you.

290. A story written within a sales letter can have a dramatic effect on your orders, especially if the "story" comes from a satisfied customer. Your prospects can relate to this type of testimonial. Another method of "personalizing" your sales letter is to put YOUR picture on it. Let the prospects see you in "action", putting orders together, getting mail out of the mailbox, etc.

291. Sales packages should include the advertising flyer, a sales letter about the book or item (if appropriate),

an order form and a return envelope. Many times the order coupon is on the advertising flyer itself or can be a separate coupon placed into the envelope.

292. When sending out sales packages, DON'T FORGET to put the "key code" from the inquirers' envelope on the Order Coupon of the advertising flyer. Simply print an "E", "Danice", "Dept. 101", etc. someplace on the order coupon - make it small but legible. Later, when that individual orders a book, you can tell immediately which advertising record sheet to record the order on because of the "key" code you've written on order coupon.

293. FREE is and always will be the most attention-grabbing word in the advertiser's dictionary. Do you know what word comes in second? "It's NEW!" Customers love to be the first to have something new. In every mailing try to announce something that customers will perceive as new. A new report, a new book, a new thing-a-ma-jig. "New" will always get the customers thinking about placing an order!

294. A good, effective act will always produce a good effect; but the effective acts must be maintained in a daily, habitual way, if we are to enjoy continual success. In other words, if one classified ad really brings in the orders, don't assume that those orders will last forever from that one ad - you must keep the ads running for continuous orders.

295. When writing a classified ad, write all the BENEFITS of your book or product, then proceed to write sentences about the benefits to your potential customers. Lay the ad aside for a day or so then come back and re-do it. Begin taking out all non-essential words, leaving the MAIN benefits. Make short sentences. Lay the ad aside for another day then come back to re-read

and maybe re-vamp it. Classified ads need to be short, to the point and use as many persuasive words as you can and still let the reader know what you are offering.

296. If you're advertising for dealers for a series of reports that you have available, instead of just using the word "free" (for FREE report, write.....) it would be to your advantage to use "sample" report (for FREE sample report, write....). This lets the reader know that they will be getting one of a larger selection of very informative reports you're making available.

297. It takes constant and consistent advertising to get your name and business to the point where it becomes "recognizable". In addition, get press releases out to as many publications as possible about your product or service and get that FREE advertising in the form of editorials.

298. DOUBLE CHECK to see that your name and address is correct on your classified ads! There is no bigger waste of money than to see your ad printed in a national magazine classified section with an incomplete or wrong address!

299. Save 17% on your advertisements! Most publications allow a 2% "cash" discount for anybody, and a 15% "agency" discount, for ads placed through an advertising agency. You can set up your own "in-house" advertising agency and receive the 15% discount. Make some letterhead with your advertising agency name (R & S Advertising Agency is ours), address and phone number and you're all set. You don't have to set up a separate bank account - just get cashier's checks or money orders to pay for the advertisement. (NOTE: The rate card in the media kit from magazines will indicate whether these discounts apply to classified advertising as well as display

advertising.)

300.   Nothing works faster or better to build a profitable business than to offer an introductory free offer. People LOVE getting something for nothing, and if your FREE offer is something useful that can promote your line of products, you will soon find your email and mailbox getting fuller and fuller of orders for the "real" items.

301.   When placing a classified ad for a particular book or item, immediately make a minimum of 50 "sales packages" that go along with what you are advertising. Even if the ad doesn't come out for a month or six weeks, you need to be prepared. It is said that delaying a week to get information out to an inquirer means a drop of 50% or more in the potential sales from that sales package.

302.   If your business is a local one, consider magnetic signs for your car or truck. And to get even more visibility, when shopping at places like Walmart, park at the end of a row, so the people driving by will also see your sign.

303.   When advertising a particular book, send only information ABOUT THAT BOOK to the inquirer. Any other books or offers you have to sell are to be used in the follow-up mailings.

304.   Don't make promises and claims in your advertising that you can't follow through with after the orders come in.

305.   Another use for the mini-flyer is to use a glue stick or tape and attach one to the back of every envelope you mail, in addition to sticking one on the lower front corner of packages that you mail. You can also use Avery

labels – 10 to a page and print your mini-flyer. Dozens of postal workers will read your "ad" as the letter or package moves to its destination!

306. Be sure to select the best classification for your ads. Pick the one that appears to be the best heading. There may be one or two other headings that you would want to "test", after the first ad. In doing a test, change only the "key code" but leave the remainder of the ad the same, in order to see which is the best.

307. Be sure to include "persuasive" words in your classified ads. The combination of many will be even better. Some of the best words include: save, money, you, new, results, easy, proven, guaranteed, FREE, discover, NOW, announcing, revolutionary, sensational, amazing, introducing.

308. Apply the **"AIDA"** principle to every ad that you place -- **A**ttention, **I**nterest, **D**esire and **A**ction. Get the readers **A**ttention, arouse their **I**nterest, create **D**esire in the reader, and ask for **A**ction (order TODAY!).

309. Strengthen your ad with "extras" that others don't mention. Do you ship the same day the orders reach you? Shout "SHIP SAME DAY" in your sales material. Let the people know if your product or book is new, hard-to-find, one- of-a-kind, first one available, natural product. If possible, give something free with orders - a free report, helpful advice, etc.

310. To be effective you must advertise on a national basis. Local "magazines" just don't bring in large enough returns for the dollars spent.

311. We suggest that you use your regular street address for ads rather than getting a Post Office box. The

fact that you use a street address makes the reader more confident in ordering -- will not even question whether you are a "fly by night" home business operator, as they might when they see a Post Office box number.

312. If you're having difficulty in deciding which of two or three classified ads to use for a particular book, ask someone to read them TO YOU. They will sound differently coming from someone else. You also might give the ads to one or two different people and ask their opinion which one is better.

313. If you are writing your own advertising flyers and sales packages, we would advise having someone edit your writing, especially at the beginning. A relative who does a lot of writing for his/her job, or a college student friend would be excellent choices.

314. Go to your public library, in the Reference Section, and ask to see the Gale Directory, which will list all current publications in print by subject. You can find all magazines in which you could possibly advertise your book or item. For more than 50 years, Gale is the trusted source for authoritative directories. www.gale.cengage.com/directoryLibrary/

315. "KEY" codes can be used with variations of your name. For example Charles Brown could be used the following ways: Brown; Charles; Chas; Chas Brown; C. Brown; Chuck; Chuck Brown. If you included your middle name in the codes it would make even more variations: "Raymond" could also be used Ray; Raymond; R. Brown; C.R. Brown; Ray Brown; Raymond Brown.

316. Because classified ads are charged by the word, get the most space for your money by using longer, but simpler, words, such as "Free information" instead of

"Free details". Spell out all words. This strategy makes your ad appear longer, takes up more lines, therefore getting more attention from the reader.

317. Start your classified ad with a strong benefit to the reader, and begin with the popular "How to..." or with an active verb, such as "get", "make", "save", "earn", buy".

318. By asking for payment in a classified ad you are gambling all of your sales effort on 20 to 35 words. With the two-step you use fewer words to entice the reader to send for your FULL sales story, which allows you to send the complete package and follow-ups as often as the profit margin allows.

319. Plan your advertising schedule (ads to place and which magazines to put them in) for 6 months to one year. Without a written plan and schedule, your home business business will never get off the ground.

320. "Marketing" your book or product involves more than just classified advertising. You need to think about good service -- get the sales letters out within 48 hours; when the orders come in, get them out within 72 hours. You need to think about "follow up" offers. The big money in home business comes from those "follow up" offers. Do you have additional books or products to offer your customer? Think about direct mail campaigns. Have you done a little homework on where to get quality name lists? Think about what advertising you want to do the next six months, the next year. If you're not prepared, deadlines will come and go and you may miss them.

321. Avoid advertising in daily or weekly publications. Monthly publications are saved, thus the advertising can produce results for years to come. We have had orders from magazine ads that were placed 10-15

years ago. SIDE NOTE: We have had the same 800 phone number since 1995, so the fact that we have moved 5 times hasn't stopped people from getting a copy of an old "Sew News" magazine and still be able to contact us.

322. Television advertising is the most powerful and authoritative mass medium. What is seen on the television screen becomes reality in the consumer's mind. Late night advertising has been highly effective for many advertisers.

323. Television viewers are passive participants who are going to get a dose of advertising whether they want to or not simply because they're on the couch watching TV.

324. A home business/internet business will succeed if the customer does not know where else to obtain certain information and is attracted by the offer in the advertisement or on your website that appears to fill the need or creates a desire.

325. If you are introducing a new product or service within the information industry, there are dozens of good publications that will publish information about your offer at no charge. You can create a "Press Release" introducing your book or product, send it to magazine editors, along with a photo of the book or product, and if the editors can see benefits for their readers may write an article about it and publish it in their magazine.

326. Don't neglect online only businesses like Quill or Viking when comparing prices for printing or office supplies. Many times online prices are much cheaper than local shops.

327. In general, people enjoy receiving all types of mail. Receiving mail gives people a good feeling, and in some cases people will request to be put on your mailing

list. We have people order something from us and specifically say "Put me on your mailing list for future mailings". Our website has a specific box where people can sign up to be on our customer mailing list.

328. NEVER go into debt to start a home business. Never use "food" or "rent" money for advertisements. If you don't have the necessary amount for a particular ad, begin today to put aside $5, $10, or $15 per week until you save the amount you need for the ad.

329. Start small in your home business. Don't go hog wild with an ad that you believe is a sure winner and put it into half a dozen publications. TEST, TEST, TEST! ALWAYS test a new ad or a re-vamped ad in one magazine and track responses before placing it in another magazine.

330. When writing your sales packages, become the prospect. Try to see life through his eyes. Adapt your writing to the kind of folks you're writing to. It will be easier to zero in on the right words that will appeal to this particular market.

331. If possible, use a **separate order blank** in your sales packages. This cuts out one step that the prospect has to take to order from you (don't have to find a pair of scissors to cut out the order form). By using a separate order form, your mailings will result in a 10% or more increase in replies.

332. Be creative in your advertising. Send for information that is advertised in the classified ads, so you can see how "everybody else" does their advertising. DON'T COPY what you receive; simply review each piece and see what you like and what "turns you off" about each one. You will be collecting "ideas" on what you can do to

make your sales packages "the best".

333. It is imperative that you get samples of what you will be selling before you start to advertise it. The actual product may not be what you "visualize" it to be, which would be the same scenario for your customers.

334. NEVER stick with an ad that does not work, even if you think it should be a winner. You will not succeed all the time in any endeavor. The trick is to make your losses small and your profits BIG.

335. Standard Rate & Data Service, Inc. (SRDS) publishes the "bible" of the mailing list business. Their huge directory is published bi-monthly, and is entitled *Direct Mail List-Rates and Data,* published by SRDS, Inc., 3004 Glenview Rd., Wilmette, IL 60091. It covers almost every mailing list available. The directories also identify the media used to obtain orders and inquiries.

336. When checking into mailing lists to rent, be sure to ask for "response" lists and not "compiled" lists. Compiled lists are all-inclusive and there is no way to determine if they have responded to offers previously or if the names were pulled from telephone books and the like. Even better, try to get people who have been "buyers" and not just "inquirers" - your possibility of making a sale is increased tremendously.

337. Inserts of various sizes included in your sales packages grab the attention of the reader and can create both excitement and sales. An "insert" can simply be a small 3"x5" reminder of your special savings: "Don't forget to call 1-800-000-0000 before (date) to receive your FREE gift". Another idea for an insert is to do a 1/2 or 1/3 sheet of paper of testimonials. Cut them apart and slip one of the testimonial inserts in each sales package.

338. A most important item to remember in your home business is that you have to separate the "suspects" from the "prospects". Suspects, or "lookers", "tire kickers", and others who only want what's FREE with no intention of ordering anything at all, must be eliminated as much as possible. This is where good, specific mailing lists come in. Make sure you're sending your offer to people who are previous buyers of products similar to yours. Your own in-house list is worth a fortune to you if you use it correctly and do mailings at least every other month to them.

339. Don't "oversell" your products in your advertising. You may get truck loads of orders if you promise the customers "the moon and the stars". But you will also get a lot of returns asking for refunds if your product doesn't measure up to what your promises.

340. Information sellers of "how-to plans", "recipes", "sources of supply", etc. are often able to get cash with order from a small classified ad. Books and manuals that are over $10 should use the two-step inquiry method of selling.

341. An important "secret" you need to know - how much to charge for your book or product. Charge too little and you won't make any profits. Charge too much and you won't make any sales. "How-to" and "Opportunity" books generally can be sold in the $15 to $25 range. Reports can run anywhere from $2 to $15 depending on the subject matter and the length of the report. The best way to "test" the price is to come up with three different prices. Make three separate sales packages with a different price in each (the remainder of the sales package is the same). Send out equal numbers of the sales packages and keep good records of the outcome. You will soon know which price is pulling the most orders, so

subsequent sales packages will have that price on it.

342. The sole purpose of your sales brochure and cover letter is to get the prospective customer to ACT - to pick up the phone and place an order, or fill out the order form and find an envelope and stamp to mail it back to you. You must read and re-read your sales material to make sure you have created enough excitement and desire within the customer to motivate them to act - NOW! After you have decided it is a great piece of work, let someone else read it and see what it does for that person.

343. There are 60 million people over the age of 50 in the U.S. and they have a combined annual personal income of over $800 Billion. This group is the most affluent in our society, owning 77% of all the financial assets in the country. Direct your thinking and your products/services toward this segment of society and it will definitely be worth your efforts!

344. Keep the names and addresses from the mail whose information and programs you're not interested in so you can turn around and send them information on what YOU have available. You already know that those folks deal in home business, so perhaps some of your information could benefit them.

345. We recommend you use colored envelopes for your sales packages, because they are attention-grabbers.

346. Getting referrals for your product or book is an ideal way to increase business at no expense of your own! If at all possible, get your customers to promote you -- give them a discount if they recommend friends to you; send along an additional advertising flyer with instructions to pass it along to a friend, etc. If your products or books are available online, get another similar website to do a

"review" of your book, and possibly a "giveaway" as well, which will get your name and your product out to many hundreds or thousands of additional people.

347. New customers are the life blood of the home business. Seek new and more creative ways to build your customer base. These good names are worth a fortune to you. Additional ways to build online customers would be with social media outlets.

348. NEVER send out sales packages printed all on white paper. BORING! Use white for the sales letter itself, then use a variety of colors for the inserts and advertising flyers that will also be enclosed.

349. Don't confuse the FEATURES and BENEFITS of your product or book. People buy, not because they NEED, but because they WANT. In order to appeal to the "wants" you MUST stress the BENEFITS, BENEFITS, BENEFITS of your product. You may have won a hundred awards, but that doesn't give one BENEFIT to the customer! There may be dozens of FEATURES of your publication but they are NOT BENEFITS. You have to tell the prospect WHY they should buy this thing! Give many and specific benefits of buying from you as opposed to buying from someone else.

350. You must convey a sincere guarantee of your book or product ("30 day money back guarantee"; "send it back for a FULL refund for up to 6 months") in your sales letter. This will let the customer know of your willingness to refund the money fully and promptly if he or she is not satisfied. The "customer satisfaction guarantee" adds a feeling of confidence and trust in you and your company, and as a matter of fact, probably less than 1% of the people will ever ask for a refund.

351. Always use words and phrases the reader will be familiar words. The "latest" word you just learned will mean nothing to a reader who has never heard of the word.

352. A two-color brochure or circular will generate more responses than a solid black type on white paper will. Color printing, however, can add considerably to your costs. We advise those just starting in home business to refrain from color printing until your sales packages and advertising flyers prove themselves by the number of responses you get from them.

353. A time saving technique for your sales packages is to design your "order card" in such a way that your mailing label can be adhered to the card, then slipped into a window envelope. By coding the "order card" or mailing label you can readily identify the source of the order more easily than with other methods.

354. Sales packages that are "hand addressed" as opposed to sticking on a label will out-pull the conventional method by 30-50%. Reason: Hand addressed envelopes look less like "advertising" and more like a personal letter. The obvious drawback here is - do you have time to do all the hand addressing of envelopes?

355. If using a coupon sale - "50% off", "Buy One Get One Free", etc., be sure to add the words "Coupon must be presented for discount", or something similar, or use a specific online promo code. This is the only way for you to track the results of your "coupon" sale.

356. Publicity doesn't just happen -- you have to SEEK it. Send press releases to home business publishers who publish home business related articles.

357. FREE publicity coming from press releases that you've sent out can bring in more sales than paid advertising. Reason: people READ editorial copy more thoroughly than plain advertising copy and tend to believe printed testimonials.

358. If you can send a photograph along with your press release, it might increase the likelihood of getting your information published.

359. A great idea for business cards is to have it printed on a Rolodex card. Customers will usually file this style card on their Rolodex, which puts it at their fingertips, instead of at the bottom of a drawer or in a trash can.

360. Positive word of mouth comments need not be left to luck. When an appreciative customer writes you with words of praise, write back to the customer and ask permission to use the statement in your advertising.

361. Negative commentary should never be left to fester. Whatever the problem is with a customer, try to rectify it immediately -- correct the problem and include an apology note along with a free item (report or something small that you sell) that will ease the tension between the customer and your company.

362. Your business card is a miniature billboard. You have to design your card so that people will keep it and refer to it often. Put as much information on it as possible so people will know WHO you are and WHERE you are.

363. ALWAYS give your customer "something extra" - it will increase the current sales as well as the future sales from that customer.

364. Never buy advertising based solely on how "cheap" it is. Select publications to advertise in based on whether they are going to reach your potential customers.

365. Generally, a "rounded" sales price for classified advertising pulls better than "fraction" pricing. For example, a $3.00 price tag would be better than $2.89 or $3.19. On the other hand for larger ticket items $49.95 sounds much better than $50.00.

366. Be sure to offer a money-back guarantee in your advertising. Statistics have shown that the longer the money back guarantee is (6 months rather than 30 days, etc.) the fewer returns there actually are.

367. STAY IN TOUCH with your BEST customers to keep them talking about you. I would encourage you to send a special "anniversary" sale flyer to your people (the anniversary of your business), thanking them for their business. In addition, for your very best customers a Christmas card will add more good-will than you could ever imagine!

368. Repeat orders from current customers is where the big home business money is. After a customer buys from you once, it is much easier to sell them something else, and then a third item or book, and so on.

369. Know who your best customers are and email or mail to them often. When someone buys from you, send them a follow-up offer 4-6 weeks later, then 4-6 weeks later send another offer (each time a different one), then do this the third time. Keep doing the follow-up offers as long as they keep buying from you. If they haven't purchased from 3 follow-up offers, take them off your "active" customer list.

370. When a person who has responded from a classified advertisement does not order from the sales package you send out, wait a month then send a second sales package promoting a DIFFERENT item or book. If the inquirer does not respond to either sales package, take him off your "active" list, and don't send anything else; they are probably just a "tire kicker", looking for FREE information.

371. Satisfied customers will make repeat purchases from you, again and again and again. Do you have a "follow-up" offer to send out to customers? A follow-up offer would include other books, additional reports or some items related to what they initially bought.

372. "Follow-up" is an extremely important part of home business. Get the sales packages out to inquirers **the next day**! Keep track of the dates of inquiries - if no order results within 30 days follow up with a second sales package advertising a different item. If an order is received from the initial sales package, make a notation of the date and send additional sales packages to the customer every 4-6 weeks until they no longer are buying, then place the name on an "inactive" listing.

7 THE MAIL ROOM

373.   Check the accuracy of your postage scales.   If the scales are not level it will not weigh accurately.

374.   Using large first class envelopes that have the green diamond border and "First Class" written inside the border will save time stamping "first class" all over a plain envelope with a rubber stamp.   It will also be much more professional.

375.   You will save a tremendous amount of money if you buy 9x12 or 11x13 envelopes that you must lick rather than the ones that have the "peel off and stick" label.

376.   Stock different size envelopes in order to have the right size for everything.   Packaging smaller items in the nearest envelope or box regardless of its size can result in an extra dollar or more in postage.   Package properly!

377.   You can exchange your old ZIP Code Directory for a new one at the post office at no cost to you or look them up at usps.com.

378. Always include advertising stuffers (catalog, circulars, advertising flyers, etc.) to get maximum return on postage charges of your outgoing orders.

379. If sending out products that require boxes, always use a reinforced filament tape for maximum protection of your parcel.

380. Investigate the benefits of getting a postage meter. It is inconvenient for small businesses to purchase every denomination of stamp (from .01 to 1.00) in order to get the exact amount of postage on packages and envelopes. By rounding it off (for example the .78 cent rate - put on 4 20 cent stamps = 80 cents; or for the $1.24 rate it might be easier to put on a $1.00 and a .32 cent stamp = $1.32) you will always LOSE a penny to 12 or 15 cents. This may seem small, but add it up over a period of a year!

381. Remember that invoices can be included in third or fourth class envelopes where correspondence cannot be included.

382. The postal service has a variety of publications that are available and a great support section at usps.com to help answer any questions that you may have.

383. It is usually best to mail your sales packages by first class mail rather than bulk mail. It is an established fact that 97% of all first class mail gets opened. Mail surveys also show that less than 80% of the bulk mail in the United States gets opened and looked at. An exception to this would be if your sales package weighs more than an ounce so that your first class postage rate would be .55 (at this printing) - it becomes almost imperative that you mail bulk (32.6 cents).

384. A real time-saver is to file the mail you need to save IMMEDIATELY! If you simply lay it on your desk for later, you may be shuffling that "file pile" a week or two from now.

385. The major disadvantage of shipping orders C.O.D. (Cash on delivery) is that it is very likely that 40% to 55% of all orders shipped will come back to you. The reason for the returns: the U.P.S. driver or mail carrier could not make delivery and get paid, or the individual has changed his mind and refuses the package.

386. If you really want to mail C.O.D., there is an extra step you can take to reduce the number of returns. A day or two before mailing the COD package, drop the customer a postcard in the mail, thanking him for the order and that the order is being processed for immediate shipment. Tell the customer you're enclosing a free (whatever you want to send), that you know he'll be thrilled with. Then say "Please be sure to have $ (total amount due) available to pay the U.P.S. driver when he comes." The prospect of something FREE in the package will increase their desire for it and they WILL be watching and waiting for your COD package!

387. NEVER mail an order to a customer without enclosing additional sales literature on products or books that you have available. This type of offer you enclose in outgoing orders is called "bouncebacks". You can expect to receive from 5% to 10% additional orders from using bouncebacks.

388. ALWAYS fold every sales letter, advertising flyer and inserts SEPARATELY. The end result should be that the contents of the letter will literally "fall" out of the envelope when the prospect opens it.

389. If you prefer that your business letters don't come to your house, you can get a "business" street address from a local "mail box service" (for example "The UPS Store").

390. Is your book or product available and ready to ship when the orders come in?   Being late in shipping your orders will cause hard feelings in your customers and will certainly keep them from ordering from you again.

391. Answer all "inquiry" letters <u>immediately</u>. When the customer wrote the letter to you, the interest in your book or product was at the highest peak. Every day after that, the interest wanes more and more until (if they don't get a response from you quickly) they are no longer interested at all.

392. Always send along an additional order form with outgoing orders - they might want to give it to a friend or buy more themselves.

393. Always send another catalog with every order. Don't just assume they already have one. The first one might have gotten misplaced, or perhaps one of the catalogs will be passed along to a friend!

394. ALWAYS open your mail on a DAILY basis.

395. Use standard sizes for your mailings. Do you know that a 6 1/2 x 9 1/2 size envelope will cost additional postage even if the "weight" would indicate one first class stamp. Reason: it is considered "oversize" and will not fit into the "slot" the postal service has regulating what is a "standard" size and what is not.

396. Compare the differences between insulated, bubble and reinforced mailing envelopes to make sure you

get what you need but not pay for more than what is necessary.

397. Establish a specific time to get outgoing mailing packages together and ready to ship - maybe the end of the day so they're ready to go out in the morning; or maybe first thing in the morning before the telephone starts to ring, etc. Set the time and stick with it day after day -- if you don't your days will come and go and you won't even think about outgoing mail.

398. Keep all Styrofoam "peanuts" or packing material that comes with orders from suppliers to be used later for your outgoing packages. If you get too much to fit into a large box, start dumping it into a large trash bag to store until you need it.

399. Many boxes and shipping containers you receive can be used again to send out your shipments.

400. When mailing out a single book we use a 10" x 13" manila envelope. Several books can be mailed in the same size "padded" envelope. If someone is ordering four or more books we ship them in corrugated "book" boxes. (A listing of suppliers can be found in the "Resources" section at the back of this book).

401. Books, manuals and reports are very easy to package (manila envelopes work great), and can be mailed at a special postal rate, as opposed to trinkets and bulky items that need special packaging.

402. If you spend your day at a computer like I do, it will be a nice change of pace to open your mail standing up. You'll find that you open the mail faster, and if there's a waste basket beside you, the "junk" mail you don't need and are not interested in can be thrown away immediately.

403. To make your bulk mail look more like first class, you can do several things: a) get bulk rate stamps rather than having the words "bulk rate" printed or stamped on your envelope, b) the mailing envelope must be a standard number 10 business size, c) don't print any "teaser" statements on the outside of the envelope, d) by just printing your return address (not the name) gives a bit more intrigue to the envelope but still allows it to retain the business look.

404. Putting a self addressed return envelope in your sales package should increase your response level by 20% or more.

405. Never put stamps on the return envelopes inside your sales package, and don't use "postage paid business reply" return envelopes. You can bet that a certain percentage of your envelopes that come back are from "cranks" or "competitors" with nothing in them.

406. Do you have questions about postal rates and policies. Contact the U.S. Postal Service at 1-800-THEUSPS for answers or go to USPS.com.

407. Keep current of changes within the Postal Service regarding mailing charges. A recent change has made the "BOUND PRINTED MATTER RATE" lower than the "BOOK RATE", at certain weights and in certain zones. When mailing books ask the postal clerk to check BOTH the "Book rate" and the "Bound printed matter" rate. There may only be small savings each time, but those savings can add up to many dollars over a years' time.

408. Is your business too small right now to benefit from bulk mail? Maybe not. Lettershops will let you use their bulk mail permit for a small fee, allowing you to send a "trial" mailing without paying for the permit and annual

fee for this test.

409. If you're having problems with orders "getting
lost in the mail", you might want to consider shipping with
United Parcel Service (UPS). All of their packages are
insured (it's part of their fee) and their deliveries are signed
for.

410. When your business grows to where you are
shipping many packages on a daily basis, get a "rate" chart
from the Post Office as well as from United Parcel Service
then compare prices for the "book rate" postal service to
the "ground" rate from UPS. If you are using UPS
consistently you can get a "business account" in which case
UPS will stop by daily to get the packages that you have.
There is a weekly charge for this service whether you have
packages to mail or not, so you will have to determine if
you have enough outgoing packages to warrant applying
for this service.

411. Keep in mind the importance of reading
carefully the mail that comes to you. Since most of your
business transactions will be done on paper (from orders
coming in to working with suppliers, etc.) if you don't pay
attention to what you're doing you could make major
mistakes. For example, a hap-hazard glance at an order
could result in sending out the wrong book, or perhaps
someone ordered two books and you only sent out one.
By the same token watch the billings of your suppliers -
they may offer a discount if you are prompt in paying.

412. Don't let your catalogs, mailings, etc. get "stale"
with the same old things month after month and year after
year. New customers won't know the difference, but it's
the old customers that you want to keep ordering from
you. Constantly be adding new and different items - even
if the items are non-related, you'll keep surprising your

customers, and your customers will keep buying!

413.   A "self-mailer" is any kind of no-envelope mailing.   This could be anything from a postcard to a catalog or flyers or brochures that are printed on heavy stock to be folded and mailed.   In a home business, we recommend that "self mailer's" NOT be used except in the case of catalogs to CUSTOMERS. You'll ALWAYS make more sales and more money using a sales letter and a flyer or circular in an envelope.

414.   Contact   your   local   Postal   Service   for information about various services. Free seminars on bulk mailing and other mail related topics are periodically offered by many postal centers.

415.   You can earn extra money from your direct marketing or home business by selling the used stamps from your incoming mail. Simply clip the stamps, allowing a 1/4" allowance around the stamps and sell to stamp dealers. Check your phone book for stamp dealers or go to your local library and look over books and periodicals that   pertain   to   stamp   collecting   -   you   will   find advertisements from stamp dealers.

416.   If you always mail in the same business size white envelope, your customers may spot it and think it's "just another mailing" and put it aside. Try using colored envelopes for a mailing, next time use window envelopes, another   time   use   a   self   mailing   catalog   -   keep   them guessing, and keep them ordering!

8 INCREASE PROFITS/REDUCE EXPENSES

417. There are two ways to make more money -- increase sales or reduce expenses. Both sales and expenses will determine the total yearend profit. Look at your total home office operation with "reduce expenses" in mind. Buying used furniture rather than new is a great "one time" savings, but we're talking about day after day expense reduction. If your business calls for the use of money orders, do you run to the nearest convenience store and pay 98 cents per money order when you could get them from your bank at no cost? (Add up 98 cents per money order times the number you'd use in a month's time and you'll know immediately how much money you'd save!) By becoming more efficient perhaps you could mail orders and meet advertising deadlines by using regular mail instead of having to use Federal Express or other "overnight" mailing services - this could save $10 to $13 dollars on each mailing!

418. The very best way to save money in a home business is to read books written by successful home

S. Denise Hoyle & Sarah J. Doyle

business experts. You can spend a little money on books such as these and learn years and years worth of tips and experience, or you can get your education by wasting perhaps large sums of money on misdirected advertising and direct mailings that bomb.

419. When you get to the point that you cannot do the work yourself, instead of hiring a full-time or even part-time employee, go to a temporary employment agency such as Manpower or Kelly. Using this method of getting outside help you're only obligated for 4 hours' work from the employee rather than "finding" work every day for a permanent person once you get caught up. We find that getting a temporary person once a week to do the filing and even typing names and addresses into the computer frees up our time so we can be marketing our products.

420. When purchasing mailing envelopes, if you'll get the kind you have to "lick" instead of the ones that are self-adhesive you can cut the cost of envelopes by half or more.

421. Don't throw away paper that's clean on one side. We keep all "recycle" paper in one stack to be used for note paper (cut it to whatever size you want), use it in your copier for "rough draft" copies, use it for the children to write and color on - there are dozens of uses for this paper which can result in the savings of at least a case of paper or more in a year's time.

422. Heavier paper for advertising flyers, sales letters, etc. could increase your postage costs. Some pieces may need heavier paper stock, but most can be done on regular 20# paper.

423. Did you know that you can buy discounted envelopes and packing supplies on eBay and Amazon?

424. You can save 50-60% on your business checks. Mail order houses like Current and Checks in the Mail can supply checks that are legal and meet the ANSI standards established by the American Banker Association.

425. Reduce expenses...Increase profits! Shop around for office supplies. Picking up a few supplies "while at the grocery store" may prove very expensive. Office supply stores are usually cheaper. And don't forget about the discount office supply catalogs.

426. Avoid printing that looks cheap. It pays off to pay a bit more to get a good job. However, do not over-pay for printing that is unnecessarily fancy for what you are doing.

427. Always give complete instructions when taking work to your printer. Leave nothing to "guess work". Know <u>exactly</u> what you want done, and put it in writing. If I'm getting books printed I make TWO lists – one for them and one for me – that says exactly how many pages are in each book and how many copies of each book that I need. We do all of our printing at Office Depot, and they know me so well that instead of writing up their form, they simply take my list and work from that.

428. Avoid special sizes and colors. Standard paper sizes and standard ink colors will always save you money.

429. Be careful in choosing the proper paper for your printing. The heavier weight papers may have a better "feel", but they will also add extra postage to your sales package.

430. Mail order is a business of details. For example, mailing the wrong way or the more expensive way, may break a program. This may sound strange, but too many

"mis-spent" dollars can eat away at any profit you might otherwise have made. "If you take care of the cents, the dollars will take care of themselves".

431. Money wasted means you have to have more sales just to make a profit. Get the most for your advertising dollar by looking for products similar to yours in various publications. If others are advertising similar products there you can be sure they are making money and so will you.

432. The printer you choose will be a prime source of good advice and a good friend if you choose one carefully. They're familiar with the many different types, weights and finishes of paper. They know what will look the best for the project you're working on. Be sure you pick someone you can trust and not have the feeling that he will tell you that you need "the expensive fancy" paper, when you know in your heart that it is not necessary.

433. Do something extra each day to perk up your business. It really pays! It may be contacting old customers, looking for ways to reach additional new customers, or researching office supply prices in order to get the best deals.

434. If possible combine several similar printing jobs for one press run. Combining several jobs, whether large or small, could save you a bundle of money. For example, I know that at Office Depot, when you reach 10,000 copies you get a huge price break, so I'll do a variety of "flyers, books, patterns" in order to reach that 10,000 mark. This makes our books much cheaper to print, flyers and patterns are much cheaper, giving a little extra "profit" on the sales end.

435. Learn to re-use and recycle as many of your

office supplies as possible. File folders can be reused simply by putting a new self-adhesive label over the old label. Scrap 8 1/2" x 11" paper can be used for first drafts of letters or sales material. Old index cards or prospect cards can be used for notes. Never throw away the paper clips from flyers or incoming mail - they also can be reused. Over a period of time the savings can be substantial by thinking of other ways to reuse and recycle!

436. The best lesson to learn concerning saving money on printing is to get lots of quotes from lots of printers. Printers are not all equal in service, quality and press room capabilities. Get a minimum of three bids on the printing job.

437. Weigh every purchase on a cost/benefit basis. This will prevent you from making unnecessary "want" purchases and keep the money for what you actually "need".

438. Always be on the lookout for additional items or books to add to your line so you will have more to sell to your customers.

439. Don't wait until the last minute to go to the printer. "Rush" jobs can mean extra charges.

9 TAXES

440. Be sure to keep track of all "business" miles for income tax purposes. Even if you're just going to the office supply store and post office, those miles add up by the end of the year. The current .56 per mile deduction that IRS allows can mean a BIG deduction for you. We suggest you get a pocket calendar, keep it in your vehicle, and on a DAILY basis write the business miles and where you went. At the end of the year, add up all the miles to use for an income tax deduction. The pocket calendar then becomes part of your tax records.

441. Did you know that if you finance your car with a home equity loan instead of a consumer loan you can deduct the interest?

442. If you're married you can legally deduct 100% of your health insurance premiums and medical expenses by hiring your spouse. Even though you (the business owner) are not eligible, your spouse (the employee) is. By selecting a health plan that includes the employee's spouse and dependents, you'll have 100% coverage. NOTE: This

may vary state by state, so be sure to check with various insurance companies and your tax professional to see what is available for you.

443. Hiring your children is an excellent way to achieve optimum tax savings. Wages earned by a child under the age of 18 are exempt from social security and Medicare taxes. A dependent child also pays zero on the first $3,700 of earned income.

444. The IRS (Internal Revenue Service) offers a variety of services, workshops and publications to clarify tax issues for business owners. Contact your local IRS office or call 1-800-829-1040 and ask for your copy of *Guide To Free Tax Services* (Publication #910). Or visit the IRS website and go to the forms and publications section

445. A manila "expando" file is perfect for keeping all your cash and paid-by- check receipts. An expando file sectioned off by "months" will work nicely. You can make labels for the various categories of receipts - "advertising", "office supplies", "postage", "telephone bills", "utility bills", "equipment purchase", etc., and place the new labels on top of the "month" separation headings. At the end of the year all receipts will already be categorized and ready to be totaled for income tax filing.

446. Contact your State sales tax office for information regarding sales tax in your state and for getting a sales tax number.

447. After totaling all expense receipts, paper clip or rubber band each category separately. Keep all receipts and copy of the tax return in a large manila envelope and mark it "Income Tax Return & Expenses, 20___". Place in a safe place and keep for 5-7 years.

448.   Keep a record of all sales transactions for yourself, as well as for the income tax paperwork.

449.   Do not try to cheat the law by not forwarding your sales tax to the proper authorities or by not paying your full share of income tax.

450.   Always keep ALL receipts, whether paying by check or with cash for end-of-year tax returns. The small .59; .75; $1.30 cash receipts can add up to many hundreds of dollars throughout the year, and without the receipts you cannot use those cash expenses as tax deductions.

10 GOAL SETTING & OTHER FACTS OF LIFE

451. There is very little difference in people, but that little difference makes a BIG difference. The little difference is **attitude**. The big difference is whether it is **positive** or **negative**. A positive attitude has a great deal to do with the success of any business!

452. Abraham Lincoln once said: "It has been my observation that people are just about as happy as they make up their minds to be." Will you make up your mind to be happy? If not, will you make up your mind not to be UNhappy?

453. Be **SMART** about your goal setting:

S Specific goals

M Measurable goals

A Achievable goals

R Realistic goals

T Time frame

454. The formula for success in a home business is very simple.

  1. Stay away from "money games" - chain letters, pyramid schemes.

  2. Get your own product.

  3. Promote it like it was going out of style.

  4. Don't give up!

455. The two most important requirements for major success are: first, being in the right place at the right time; second, doing something about it!

456. It is very important that you set goals for your business. Short term goals, intermediate goals, and long term goals. What do you want to have done by next week? next month? Where do you want to be 5 years from now? If you have no WRITTEN goals, your business will go NOWHERE! How will you know if you have moved ahead in your business? Are you moving at all? Only with written goals will you know if you are moving ahead and the pace in which you are moving.

457. The 80/20 rule applies to running a home based business. Eighty percent of your results usually come from 20 percent of your efforts. It's imperative to have a clear perspective of what you want to accomplish.

458. Don't confuse "activity" with "accomplishment". Being busy doesn't mean you're accomplishing anything. Are you "looking" for something

you've misplaced? Are you handling inquiry mail and email half a dozen times when one daily routine would take care of it?

459. A burning desire is the greatest human motivator of all. Desire and determination are key elements in achieving success! The more you think about your goals, the more enthusiastic you become. Enthusiasm turns your "desire" into a "burning desire", which can turn your dreams into realities!

460. Probably the one human trait which stands out above all others as an aid to success is the fixed habit of turning on MORE will power instead of quitting when the going becomes hard and defeat seems eminent. Determine what you want most from life. Adopt that as your definite major purpose. Make the start toward your goal right where you stand. When you come to those uphill pulls where the going is hard, back it with all the enthusiasm at your command and you will find yourself on the right path.

461. Good health demands at least eight hours sleep a day for most people. Eight to ten hours a day are required for work. This leaves from six to eight hours a day of "free time" which one may use as he pleases. This is the most important part of the day, as far as your personal achievement is concerned. You can read self-improvement or opportunity books. You can dabble in writing a book or getting involved in a home business. You can watch television or play computer games or spend the time shopping - the choice is yours. Napoleon Hill once stated "The person who uses his free time solely for personal pleasure and play will never be a success at anything". Think about it!

462. Make a commitment to follow through on your

plan and strategy regardless of the obstacles or setbacks. "Winners never quit, and quitters never win!" Perseverance will take you to the top!

463. Don't be afraid to make mistakes. If you never dare to risk a mistake, your initiative, your creativity, and even your powers of logical thought will finally wither and die.

464. Whatever you do, do it to the BEST of your ability!

465. The key to happiness is having dreams, and the key to success is making those dreams come true.

466. Did you know that by relying on someone else for a paycheck you have a better chance of being struck by lightning than to see your income double by age 42?

467. Remember this - the only difference between the successful person and the unsuccessful person is that the successful person goes ahead and does what the rest of the crowd just talks about!

468. Someone once said that success is 99% perspiration and 1% inspiration. We agree. That 1% inspiration is the spark, the genius, behind any endeavor. Without it, nothing would ever get done. Dreams would never become reality, in fact, there would be no dreams. While willingness to work hard is crucial to the success of any good plan, without that tiny spark of inspiration there would never be a plan.

469. All of your successes and your failures are the results of the habits you have formed. There are two types of habits - those which we form deliberately and voluntarily for definite purposes, and those which we

permit to be formed by the chance circumstances of life through LACK OF AN ORGANIZED philosophy or work plan by which to provide an ordered life. Therefore we can control our earthly destinies and our way of living only to the extent that we control our thoughts and change our habits.

470. Ideally, "free time" should be divided into several parts -- some of it to self-improvement, some to recreation and relaxation, some to a hobby. It is the "hobby" and "self-improvement" segments that could be the beginning of a prosperous home business venture for you.

471. Your time is one of your greatest assets! It is the one asset you can change into any form of riches you choose. Or you spend your entire lifetime without a plan or purpose beyond that of earning enough money to survive.

472. 85% of your success depends on how DETERMINED you are to do whatever it takes to turn your dreams into a reality!

473. Get at least three bids on all your printing job. There can be a tremendous difference in charges between printers. Check around until you are satisfied with the printer and the price.

474. Don't listen to outsiders who want to either "do you a favor" or "save you money". Don't listen to advice from family and friends who will try to talk you out of getting started in your business. We would recommend that you don't even tell them (except your spouse) what you are doing to keep down the obvious negative thoughts and advice.

475. Learn to evaluate your own skills and abilities and how to set attainable goals. Start with one or two small goals that can be accomplished in a day or two, then set a couple more goals that can be accomplished in a few days. There's a tremendous feeling of pride as you see your goals being accomplished. Move forward with larger goals. You will be amazed at how easy it is to set and work toward attaining those goals when you get in the habit of doing something constructive EACH DAY.

476. Be a doer instead of a sitter. Participate actively rather than just sit back and wait for something to happen. The get-up-and-go attitude will be a big factor in whether your business will succeed or not.

477. Have confidence in your own value. Self respect, self worth, and self liking go a long way toward building self confidence. You must consider yourself and your information to be of value to the other person.

478. It's amazing how much more can be accomplished in a day if you get up 30 minutes earlier than usual.

479. The only way to get rid of a bad habit is to **replace** it with a good habit. Rather than concentrate upon what you are not going to do, concentrate on what you ARE going to do. Making a determined effort "not to do something" reinforces it instead of preventing it.

480. The more optimistic you are, the more likely you are to succeed.

481. To form the habits you want to form, use mental imagery. Create a "picture in your mind" of the desired end-result and then concentrate upon what needs to be done in order for the "picture" to come to life. The

very act of picturing yourself reaching your goal is a good habit to replace negative ones.

482.   It takes 21 days to form habits.   After this amount of time, we get to the place where the thing we have been practicing and working on actually becomes a part of us.

483.   Form habits consistent with the person you want to be.   Our habits determine our physical, mental, emotional and spiritual successes.   Our habits lead to wins or losses.   We are the sum result of our habits.

484.   Enthusiasm is contagious.   Choosing to look at the world with enthusiasm, confidence and a sense of humor is a choice YOU must make.   Avoid pessimists - they can poison life and your outlook on life!

485.   Life gives to us what we are willing to work for! Forget the "get rich quick" schemes and "big dollars for doing nothing" opportunities -- they are NOT opportunities!   We've all been given a formula for success since creation "Do unto others as you'd have them do unto you" and "give and it shall be given unto you" are only two of the many principles we all should be living by.

486.   Planning your business venture is a three-step process: 1) setting specific goals and objectives; 2) writing out the methods, techniques and timetables necessary to reach the goals and objectives; 3)   keeping accurate assessment of progress that's being made and doing some adjusting if necessary.

487.   74% of all American millionaires own their own business.   The first day you start a home-based business you instantly TRIPLE your chances of financial independence.

488. People who fail to achieve their goals are usually "deficiency- motivated", or focused on what's MISSING from their lives instead of focusing on what they are CAPABLE OF ACHIEVING.

489. It is very important to sell only stuff that you are proud to sell. No one can achieve long term success who sells something that he or she is not proud of.

490. You'll always miss 100% of the shots you don't take! What separates successful people from everyone else isn't superior strength or knowledge, but an indomitable will to succeed, and a methodical, efficient game plan.

491. The so-called "great" people are only normal everyday people who grabbed a great idea before it disappeared into oblivion.

492. Five simple steps to success: 1) Dream BIG dreams; 2) Set objectives (goals) on how to make those big dreams come true; 3) Develop a plan (those who fail to plan, plan to fail); 4) Commit yourself - make a commitment TODAY to do something that will make your big dream come true; 5) Believe in yourself - by believing you CAN do this thing, you WILL do it!

493. Two important facts of life stand out boldly. One is that defeat in some form inevitably overtakes each of us, at one time or another. The other is that every adversity brings the seed of an equivalent or greater benefit, often in some hidden form. Remember whenever a "door" closes on us, (in the form of a failure, defeat, job loss, etc.) another "door" opens - it is up to us to find that "open door".

494. Remember these words: Nothing in the world can take the place of persistence. Talent will not; nothing

is more common than unsuccessful men with talent. Genius will not; unrewarded genius is almost a proverb. Education alone will not; the world is full of educated derelicts. Persistence and determination alone are omnipotent!

495. Some important words of wisdom I've read and are absolutely true... "Don't hire friends, don't borrow money from friends!" The same thing holds true for relatives.

496. Never forget - someone is waiting to buy what you are selling!

497. THOUGHTS determine what you want....ACTION determines what you get!

498. A practical way of solving your challenges and problems is to list the challenges, problems and anxieties. Rather than becoming frustrated, angry and anxious and becoming overwhelmed with challenges, take the time to write down every problem. The very act of listing the challenges will give clarity on what they are and you can then put them in perspective. Learning to recognize frustration and fears before becoming overwhelmed is the first step in resolving them.

499. Life is not a spectator sport! All the knowledge in the world won't help you if you don't take action. Do you have the courage to get started changing your life? Where will you be next year, in five years, or ten years from now if you continue doing what you're doing? How many more years will you work for someone else, ensuring THEIR financial success? Dreams only come true if the desire is great enough for you to take action NOW.

500. Don't worry about the competition. Mind your

own business and make your business the best possible - best products, best books, best service - and your business will grow and thrive!

501.   J. Paul Getty once wrote: It shouldn't be difficult for anyone to *resist the temptation* to allow himself to get into the pattern of being average.   One needs only to remember that a groove may be safe -- but as one wears away at it, the groove becomes first a rut and finally a grave.   Why not see what you can really do -- how far you can go?   Why not become the most you can and really live life instead of just watching it pass by?   Someone once said there are three kinds of people: those who MAKE things happen, those who WATCH things happen, and those who WONDER what happened.   Which are you?

11 DISCLAIMER

In this book, the author and publisher have tried to get you enthused about starting your own business, or taking your current business to the next level. However, you must realize that the possibility of failure is a fact of life in the business world. There is no business on this earth where everybody succeeds (if there were such a business, every person in America would immediately quit their current job and go into that business).

There are many, many variables, any one of which could make your business venture show little or no profit. Your own initiative and desire will play the greatest part in whether your business will be a success. We remind you that nothing printed in this book should be interpreted as a guarantee, on the part of the author or the publisher, that your business will be profitable.

All of the information in this book reflects the opinions of the author. While we believe that the information is accurate as of the date of printing, it is possible that there are errors of omission.

This book is not intended to give legal or financial advice, since neither the author nor the publishers are accountants or attorneys. Whenever you need such advice, you must consult a professional lawyer or accountant, or both.

This book is simply a guide for you to follow as you get your business up and running. The purpose of this book is to give you a better "handle" on your business venture by offering tips and strategies in the various areas of your home business. Many times in a new business the small things are overlooked, and every detail, whether large or small is important to a profitable business.

Because you are the boss of your business, it will be up to you to motivate yourself to do the necessary work to remain in business.

12 RESOURCES

http://youcanworkathomenow.com/ ~ Work at home tutorials – helping you make money online!

http://SewWithSarah.com ~ Your pattern and pattern making headquarters!

http://PlusSizeChildren.com ~ Patterns, classes, books and links that make it easier to sew for plus size children!

http://PatternsThatFitYou.com ~ The online fashion design school teaches the art of custom fitting patterns and pattern making to beginners and experts alike.

http://Patterns2Go.com ~ A variety of patterns to choose from – sewing, crafting, knitting, crochet, tatting, and more.

http://SewMachineRepair.com ~ Learn how to repair your own treadle, serger and sewing machines and save yourself time, money and frustration.

http://CouponClutch.com ~ Carry your coupons in one of these fashionable fabric covered 3 ring binders.

http://WomInfo.com ~ The go-to site for women in business, or who want to be in business.

http://ShopperStrategy.com ~ Be a better shopper! Tips and reviews from a frugal shopper.

http://SewingBusiness.com ~ Information plus tutorials for those who sew and for those in the business of sewing for others.

ABOUT THE AUTHORS

Sarah J. Doyle ~ Pattern Maker, Instructor & Author
Sarah learned to make patterns from her own measurements through a Chinese interpreter at a local pattern making school while her husband was stationed in Taiwan for the Air Force. Her friends all wanted her to teach them once she got the hang of it so she wrote up instruction manuals and began teaching classes more than 30 years ago. She now has over twenty books she's written on custom patternmaking techniques, sewing businesses, and other sewing topics, as well as several lines of custom specialty patterns.

You can also visit Sarah at her personal blog http://sarahjdoyle.com, or learn more about her pattern making techniques at http://patternsthatfityou.com and http://sewwithsarah.com.

S. Denise Hoyle ~ Author, Instructor & Pattern Designer
Denise is Sarah's daughter and she learned much about sewing and pattern design from her mother while growing up. She started her own business in high school and made extra money sewing for people and doing alterations from home for other businesses like local dry cleaners. Denise later also became interested in creating patterns and has since authored a number of specialty sewing books. While sewing is Denise's first love, the world of electronic commerce also fascinates her, and that interest led her to pursue a Masters Degree in eBusiness and Technology. Now Denise spends her time teaching business subjects to online college students, in addition to sharing her love of sewing with others through classes, instructional books, and unique pattern designs.

Learn more about Denise at http://denisehoyle.com, or check out some of her pattern designs at http://patterns2go.com.